ON SERIOUS EARTH

POETRY & TRANSCENDENCE

ON SERIOUS EARTH

POETRY & TRANSCENDENCE

BY DANIEL TOBIN

ORISON
BOOKS

ISBN: 978-1-949039-03-0

Orison Books
PO Box 8385
Asheville, NC 28814
www.orisonbooks.com

Distributed to the trade by Itasca Books
1-800-901-3480 / orders@itascabooks.com

Cover image courtesy of Shutterstock.

Manufactured in the U.S.A.

ORISON
BOOKS

CONTENTS

ACKNOWLEDGMENTS

Selections from these essays first appeared, in somewhat different form, in *Berfrois* and *Alabama Literary Review*. I also want to thank Christine Casson, Luke Hankins, Joan Houlihan, Andrew Latimer, Barbara Ras, and William Thompson for their early readership and editorial suggestions.

In memory of Nathan A. Scott, Jr.
and for my students.

Around the throne of God, where all the angels read perfectly, there are no critics—there is no need for them.

–Randall Jarrell

PREFACE: WHAT IS THE ANSWER?

I was born in a city of bridges. Where Walt Whitman's Brooklyn ferry once conveyed crowds of men and women attired in the usual costumes above the flood-tide, Roebling's Gothic masterpiece rose like a stone and steel cathedral between Fulton Park and the South Street Seaport. As I grew older it became Hart Crane's Bridge, his "harp and altar of the fury fused," its synoptic arc symbolizing an "Everpresence beyond time." Such outrageous poetic ambition—synergies, pervasive Paradigms! Alongside, the workmanlike trestles of the Manhattan Bridge, its subway lines and hemmed-in roadways, offered a worldly vision, like the Williamsburg further on connecting the teeming immigrant streets on one side of "the river that is East" to the other. When I was very young someone wrote a song about the 59th Street Bridge— *Slow down, you move too fast* . . . . Sometimes, to leave the city northward my father would drive us over the curve-ship of the Triboro, renamed now after the murdered brother of an American President. In our Rambler we would lift off from the deep trench of the Brooklyn Queens Expressway, having taken the grated hill of the Kosciuszko Bridge, named for the Polish patriot, linking the two boroughs. Or our journey might have been through the Palisades over the cross-hatched girders of the George Washington, or the Whitestone, or the endlessly flung-over armature of the Throgs Neck into the Bronx, Hart's Island with its pauper's cemetery and mass graves below us at the meeting of the river and the Sound. Most of these latter bridges were conceived and built by a man named Moses. He built the bridge I watched as a child, rising above the apartment buildings where Shore Road met Third Avenue—the Verrazano-Narrows, a giant's legs vaulting upwards with those of his twin across the strait.

Though I would not have understood so back then, the bridges that marked off the city of my youth were at once definers of boundaries and way-crossings beyond the roughhewn conglomeration of neighborhoods that shaped our sense of identity. Or should I say senses, identities? I grew up on one street, in one parish among others in one neighborhood in one borough that was nominally a part of The City, beyond which in every direction—states, country, nations, a world. Any farther context for life and lives also cam from Apollo moonshots, television, movies—a solar system, a galaxy, galaxies, a universe. Are these widening circles of reference connected as by a network of bridges, or do they exist apart from any binding relationship? Or are they merely One Vastness in which the particulars—lives, experiences, localities— are subsumed beyond any real definition? As Diotima instructs Socrates in Plato's *Symposium,* everything in life manifests the condition of being *metaxu,* a middle ground, intermediary, a bridge, to the beautiful and the good—the immortal, that "everlasting loveliness which neither comes nor goes, that neither flowers nor fades."[1] Some twenty-four hundred years later the French philosopher Simone Weil invoked her Greek predecessor when she declared "the essence of created things is to be intermediaries. They are intermediaries leading them from one thing to another and there is no end to this. They are intermediaries leading to God."[2] The fundamental problem for Weil is that we no longer know created things are bridges, that everything within the power of human creation has the ideal condition of being a bridge. It is an insight Hart Crane knew when he envisioned his Bridge, Roebling's actual structure of steel and stone, the symbol of an Everpresence—Diotima's everlasting Loveliness that neither comes nor goes. With space, time is metaxu, intermediary, the bridge, the separation that is likewise the medium of communication, and ideally of communion with what transcends. This is a vision of possibility that feels as though it is passing away, has been passing away for some time, if it has not passed away already.

Often when I walk the streets of the city where I live now I come across a church under construction, though it is not a church newly being constructed but a building being constructed out of the church, or what was a church before it had been sold to developers and undergone the requisite desacralizing ritual. Nowadays the buildings I notice are condominiums, often luxury condominiums that have left the old stonework of the façade intact, having disassembled the interior—the pews, missals, perhaps the paintings and sacred statues sold at auction or scattered to antique stores. Perhaps someone right now is sitting in one of the pews, cushioned, in the new game room of their house. The old 19th-century church I walked past last week had been the imposing center of the first German-speaking parish in Boston's South End. I had walked by many times before, though the services had long ceased and the doors were bolted. The church has become a shell, something akin to the building Philip Larkin encounters in his great poem "Church Going." Though there is no going inside this one any longer, the windows gone, the roof, the walls propped with steel, the backhoe parked alongside where the company will sink the foundation and raise the glossy, reflective glass stories around the gray stones workers will steam-blast clean. No, not a "special shell" any longer, nor empty, not that; more like a fossil shell fragmented into another, dissimilar context. In Larkin's poem, despite the faithlessness of the poet and the absence of worshippers, the church sustains nonetheless—"A serious house on serious earth it is / In whose blent air all our compulsions meet, / Are recognized and robed as destinies."[3] Such a building, he reflects even in his grudging way, can never be obsolete. It, too, remains a bridge—a point of departure, the threshold of a crossing.

"The starting point of poetry, like that of religion," Octavio Paz reflects in *The Bow and the Lyre*, "is the original human situation—being there, knowing we have been thrown into that *there* that is the hostile and indifferent world."[4] Poetry, like Weil's metaxu or Larkin's church, is originally where all our compulsions meet and are recognized, where (however threadbare) they are robed as destinies. Written more than forty years ago, the great Mexican poet's extended meditation on the nature of what he calls "the poetic revelation" might be regarded as a much belated Romantic's nostalgic effort to cling to a vision of reality that has long passed away, like the idea of a centered universe or the human soul. Given our own even more skeptical time, for a figure of the soul let a flat screen buzz and hum with infinites of information chatted or tweeted in elevators and gas stations, or in the palm of your hand, momentarily amusing, shocking, appalling, entertaining, and easing one away distractedly into a self-enwound world apart that masquerades as part of a world.

Paz, of course, had already foreknown the technologically opulent but spiritually compromised world of our 21st century. Yet he believed technology offered no vision for the future. For Paz, any future is founded on what he calls otherness, otherness that antecedes history, technology, religion, poetry, and even love. For Paz, otherness lies in the experience of the divine, an experience "more ancient and original than any religious conception."[5] Poetry comes before religion, both ontologically and historically, but the other, the essential Otherness—Diotima's Immortal, Crane's Everpresence—comes before poetry. It is what Weil nearer our own time, like Plato long ago, regarded as the basis for all metaxu, all bridges. "The beginning," Paz declares, "is not historical nor is it something that belongs to the past, but it is always present and ready to be incarnated . . . . History is the place where the poetic word is incarnated."[6] Though the world has become nothing more than a "cluster of objects and relations" viewed from a wholly subjective, wholly immanent perception of consciousness, poetry remains "a longing . . . to establish an enduring realm" without which there is no human imagining, no poetry, no soul, and no transcendence.[7]

Paz makes claims for poetry that Weil would recognize and embrace: the poetic word incarnated in history. Larkin, of course, being one of "the less deceived," perhaps not so much. Paz certainly conceives of poetry in ways that would make the populist atheism of our own time recoil, beholden as it is to the wholly materialist conception of life that has become pervasive over the past several hundred years. Then again, as Paz recognized, Western atheism is simply another kind of faith—an "anti-theism" very different from the non-theological religious practice of Buddhism, and as passionately held as any fundamentalism. Notwithstanding anti-theism's rootedness in its own belief requirements, one must acknowledge belief systems (religious or otherwise) often fall far short of ethical ideals. When they become ideologies, they fall even farther into repression, and worse. Yet despite our daily intake of suppression and regression, all of those consuming "ideas of order" with their penchant in the extreme for self-engendering violence, terror, and exploitation, there remains, if only at the periphery, the core experience of the spiritual, intuited fleetingly in everyday encounters—gestures of kindness, natural beauty, art, adherence to the core aspiration of faith despite genuine doubt and misgivings in the outward signs of belief. If, as Paz believes, religion is an interpretation of an original otherness laid like a bridge over poetry's prior encounter with what transcends our finite knowing, then the textures of religion with their implicit endorsement of the analogical—time staked in meaning through the valorizing embrasures of eternity—can remain vital to the practice of poetry even in our own deeply skeptical and fractious time.

"Time is for man, not man for time," reflected the author of *The Cloud of Unknowing*, the classic mystical text written in the fourteenth century, the name of its author lost with the other victims of plague in Europe's late medieval biological apocalypse. Our being is *of* time but not ultimately *for* time. Nearly six centuries later, Simone Weil echoed the insight: "The world is the closed door. It is a barrier. And at the same time, it is the way through."[8] The barrier is also a bridge. It would be disingenuous of me if I did not acknowledge I favor poetry that bridges the nexus where the profane and sacred cross, poetry that continues to celebrate "the impulse toward transcendence"[9] in a seemingly un-redeeming world. This book is an exploration of that nexus. It assumes, among other things, that "the greatest works of literature pull against a powerful sense of causality."[10] Though this is not a book of craft essays like those that have proliferated in recent years, it does offer close readings of poems, but does so in service of the more emphatic aim of plumbing the aesthetic and ontological questions that underlie the practice of poetry in our time. That practice for the most part finds itself embedded in a prevailingly materialist and increasingly nominalist culture—a culture long on "connectivity" and short on true bridges. Nicholas Carr has incisively called this culture "the shallows," and in those shallows he claims we have come to experience "a reversal of the early trajectory of civilization" from "cultivators of personal knowledge" to "hunters and gatherers in the electronic data forest."[11] This book contests that culture, its impact on poetic practice, as well as certain assumptions of practice that have evolved over time within what would appear to be a hastening trajectory away from the claims of depth and meaning.

In addition, while *On Serious Earth* does not presume to be a work of theology, it does rely on the kind of theological analysis given, for example, by Stephen Fields in his excellent *Analogies of Transcendence: An Essay on Nature, Grace, and Modernity*. As Fields observes, the whole enterprise of metaphysics "finds little sympathy in today's agnosticism about universal truth claims."[12] *On Serious Earth* assumes the unavoidable relevance of metaphysical questions to the art of poetry, though our "metaphysically representational" culture has been progressively undermined. With it, as Fields reflects, goes "nature's congenial participation in the uncreated" without which transcendence ceases to be "the guarantor of meaning."[13] Without this guarantor poetry finds itself awash in the shallows, distracted by the endless play of surfaces. In contrast, I confess to prizing poems that exhibit a "yearning intellect," that exhibit a desire for "the pre-apprehended absolute" in which the transcendent remains "an ingredient in reality."[14] On the other hand, the conviction that "belief in meaninglessness . . . offers a richness and success that is mirrored and abetted by the language of meaning and belief"[15] carries little weight here, though it may have currency. Any "belief in meaninglessness" pretends to an ersatz transcendence, which makes that belief self-contradictory, or equivocation. This does not mean good work and even great work cannot be achieved in the face of meaninglessness— witness Larkin's magnificently unsparing "Aubade." It does mean that the drive for meaning and its necessity for making inevitably undergirds any "belief in meaninglessness," especially for writers who "see fracture and materialism not as ends in themselves but as the condition of transcendence."[16] There can be no transcendence without the pre-condition, unquestionably paradoxical, of some condition-less guarantor of meaning.

From this standpoint language should be understood fundamentally as metaxu, metaphor, a bridge, and not a system of discretely atomized signs, from the Greek "metaphora," a transference or carrying over. To say as much is to favor an idea of order that binds together unity and difference—an analogical order. Poetry at bottom is metaphor, and there can be no metaphor without analogy, for without the analogical imagination the world is islanded into fragments that bear no real relation to each other. In such a world bridges are impossible, mediation is impossible, for the world is conceived in wholly equivocal terms. In such a world, nothing exists in the same sense, everything is "completely diverse from everything else."[17] In a contrarily univocal world all things exist uniformly, they have no real character, no real individuality. Both the equivocal and the univocal are finally reductive; the first makes language a dissociative playground, while the second allows it to succumb to a sort of mental and social fascism where lies can become alternative facts for the sake of the one reality that counts. Both lock us in a universe without ontological, much less metaphysical, bridges. Only the analogical embodies the intermediary ideal, the middle ground, the hope of genuine connection and communication across equally real differences, not to mention the hope of transcendence. Only with the analogical are language and reality safeguarded, and the poet's work enlivened with mediatory and not just mechanical power.

The art of poetry at its most necessary is a work of longing, a harkening to an answer that is poetry's essential impetus and end. Such a claim for poetry harkens back to Diotima's idea of Love in Plato's *Symposium* as the longing for immortality, yes, despite Plato's protestations against poets as corruptors of his ideal Republic—imitators of a world already at a remove from the ideal, eternal Forms. What is the answer? It is only by broaching the question seriously that we begin to build the bridge, such that the bridge comes to embody the answer posited in the very act of crossing over. Poems at their most necessary however multifarious in form and expression consciously provoke our assent to the possibility of an answer. By bridging meaning's audacious and familiar passage over the meaningless, poetry comes to place us again on serious earth, and so awakens the always nascent and doggedly immanent hunger for transcendence that is never obsolete. On serious earth, we recognize, in Teilhard de Chardin's words, "the supreme improbability, the tremendous unlikelihood" of finding each other and ourselves "existing in the heart of a world that has survived and succeeded at being a world."[18]

ON DISSENSUS, OR THE LOSS OF TRUE NORTH

1. *The Hall*

In one of my albums of old family photographs there is a picture of my brother and me standing on either side of Babe Ruth's locker in the Baseball Hall of Fame. I am eleven, my brother two years older, and we look the part for the time: 1969, the sons of stolid Irish Catholic parents who had us in the late 1950s, still button-down and Brill-creamed that summer of Civil Rights and Woodstock and kill counts from Vietnam before our tepid teenage rebelliousness kicked in, incongruously, in the era of the Hustle and the platform shoe. In another photograph, we are joined by our mother's childhood friend, Connie, a nun in full regalia, her rosary a beaded lasso looped at her side, her face crimped but smiling broadly under her snood's high white façade—her habit's equally constricted and flowing architecture preserved now in the photograph beside the exalted uniforms. By then I had memorized the batting averages, home runs, and other salient statistics of the all-time leaders as well as the dimensions of every major-league ballpark, past and present. I kept my current baseball cards in a special plastic case designed to look like a miniature locker complete with swinging doors. Now I was roaming exaltedly in the Museum's sacred space among the holy relics of the greatest of the game's greats. Even Connie with her strange uniform familiar to me after six years at St. Anselm's offered a surprising vantage—an encounter with the ordinary human, unimposing, behind the remoter, sterner visages I knew daily during my formative years at school. For me, it was the best vacation ever. Now, in the widened context of forty-odd years, it is a moment of unapologetic innocence unrecoverable except by a kind of artful conjuring that is itself furthered as much by the inevitability of distance as by the approximations of memory.

Though my early-life fascination with baseball's numbers compulsion—as an almost mythological measure of achievement—has waned considerably with age, I find myself taken up by the current contentious deliberations over who belongs in the Hall of Fame from among recent players—who, in a phrase, measure up in their own time and state of the game to the legendary greats, and do so without performance enhancing drugs, or in spite of an array of issues from equipment to rules to institutionalized racism that make it less than optimal to discern real greatness across the eras. It is fortunate, nonetheless, despite the occasional disagreement, that by and large the Baseball Hall of Fame has a firm intuition of exemplary performance and inducts new generations of "the great" onto its plaques in those vaguely Parnassian halls on the shores of Lake Otsego in upstate New York. Likewise, it maintains a firm grasp of tradition, the history of the game with all of its changes, idiosyncratic characters great and otherwise, and exceptional moments; which makes individual greatness only one aspect, albeit a crucial aspect of the idea of tradition. Still, if one browses the Internet one can find a by now famous photograph of the first inductees—Ty Cobb, Walter Johnson, Babe Ruth—the standard of greatness against which all future players would be measured.

Seeing the photograph of the first inductees reminded me of my long-ago visit to the Hall that summer. The image came to mind again when I viewed another iconic photograph from a decade or so later of poets at a reception in the Gotham Book Mart: W.H. Auden, Elizabeth Bishop, Marianne Moore, Delmore Schwartz, Randall Jarrell, Stephen Spender, all framed by tall, crowded stacks of books. Auden, his face still smooth and youthful, not the craggy, melting Rushmore it would become over the next thirty years, perches precariously on a ladder hovering above in a kind of private Olympus. Elizabeth Bishop stands demurely below, tight-lipped, one white glove, and looks as if she's waiting in trepidation for the immigrant bard to tumble down from his high empyrean. In front of Bishop sits Marianne Moore, warm and prim and satisfied, looking straight into the camera, unlike Randall Jarrell to her left (incorrectly captioned with Delmore Schwartz) who appears to have spotted a small rodent just outside the frame. Or is he thinking of World War II? Or has he an idea for a poem about a woman in a grocery store who regrets her life, which is really his life? Delmore Schwartz sits beside him, leaning forward, and seems to be imploring the photographer to please take the shot now so he can escape to the nearest tavern. A young phenomenon, in eighteen years he'll die alone in a flea bag hotel in New York. It will take the morgue two days to identify the body. Across the room seated on a chair back, the ever-aquiline Stephen Spender looks out with what appears to be total equanimity at some distant point in the receding universe somewhere in the stacks between Jarrell and Moore. Here are many of the Poetry Game's near greats or greats. Others are in the frame, noteworthy in their day but less regarded now, if not nearly forgotten: the Sitwells, Edith and Osbert, sitting quite well together close to the center of the room as though they alone were the focus of the shot; Horace Gregory, Richard Eberhart, Marya Zaturenska, José Garcia Villa, Charles Henri Ford, William Rose Benét, already looking like a sad neglected uncle despite having won the Pulitzer Prize. Not all writers here are poets: Tennessee Williams and Gore Vidal stand in back appearing vaguely bemused. Who should be sitting up front in the one empty chair? Robert Frost—snowbound in Vermont? Wallace Stevens, dreaming of Key West? Ezra Pound? But he's been taken from his Italian cage to a room in the "bedlam" of St. Elizabeth's. Robert Lowell? John Berryman? Langston Hughes? Louise Bogan? Theodore Roethke? Stanley Kunitz? Robert Hayden? Gwendolyn Brooks? Against the back wall on the shelf's reflective glass the camera flash explodes in silent reverb like a sudden glimpse of quantum expansion.

Or is it quantum compression? Poetry anthologies, one might propose, are akin to snapshots. They give an image of the art at a particular moment in time, though unlike snapshots they carry presumptions of artistic timelessness. In turn, to browse web and blog commentaries on contemporary poetry is to encounter an enormous variety of reflections on the state of the art, some cogent, others vitriolic in the way permissible within a medium that thrives by leveling hierarchies. The most intelligent of these discussions raise the undeniable issue of "dissensus" in contemporary poetry, as well as "the problem of multitude" in what really looks to be a quantum expansion of individual voices and schools. There is just so much poetry being written that it is impossible to keep up, much less determine "the best" poems and poets of our time. More than confusion, the sheer multitude of poetry produced implies a flattening of standards. How does one judge what is good much less what might eventually be recognized as "Hall-worthy?" As one commentator observed: "the kind of writing you like is just one kind of potentially valuable writing." The issue raised by poetry dissensus, though potentially easily dismissed as incidental to the times, in fact betrays a deeply seated problem since it demonstrates how the current historical and cultural moment shapes our views of the past, and thus shapes the future of the art—at least the immediate future.

Within this broadened context one can elaborate a few principles of selection. The first might be called invoking the established standards of greatness, the best of the best, advancing an elite to be inducted into the "poetry Hall" based on the complexity of stylistic achievement. In this view, great poets simply by being great must be few in number. The charge against such a view would be elitism. Conversely, strictly established standards of merit may play second to the capacity for poems to "illuminate the times in which they were crafted."[19] In the first case, style evinces a kind of timelessness across history and cultures. Greatness, if not self-evident, is discernable by those who have the capacity to discern greatness. Anthologies are definers of taste, they are ventures for identifying enduring worth, and therefore they must take style and complexity principally if not exclusively into account. This might be called a gatekeeper model of editorship and tradition. In the alternate model, history and cultural change inevitably shape literary merit, style, and may be said to infuse a meritorious poem with the required complexity that warrants its inclusion. Aesthetic value as a category of judgment becomes a subspecies of historical value. Worthiness, if not greatness, is as much a production of the historical moment, the culture and politics of the time as it is of the poet who made the poem. Any anthology must therefore take account of evolving practices and influences. Such a model leaves the door open for historically representative poems especially if they track cultural and sociological trends. Underwriting this view is the assumption that a poem's historical significance encodes the desired aesthetic gravitas. Yet all one needs to do in this model, as Frank Kermode reminds us, is to consider history "a fictive substitute for authority and tradition, a maker of concords between past, present, and future, a provider of significance to mere chronicity . . . . Everything is relevant if its relevance can be invented, even the scattered informations of the morning newspaper."[20] These two conceptions of how to preserve what is valuable in the art suggest seriously different understandings of tradition and canon-making. This clash of conceptions raises further questions about the cultural and historical conditions of taste, and the continued relevance of tradition and canon-making for the future of the art.

2. *Handing Over and Measuring Up*

For all of the ephemeral critical heat generated by recent discussions of editorial favor, the concerns raised about critical judgment and the cultivation of tradition are nothing new. There may be no disputing taste, as Horace continues to remind us some two thousand years after his death, though that fact hasn't prevented disputes from shaping not only what comes into favor at a certain moment in history but also what is given a moniker of enduring value despite the culture's shifting claims. On what, presumably, does one base one's principle of selection, and therefore for "induction"? The admittedly tongue-in-cheek analogy between investiture into the Hall of Fame and selection into any anthology that claims to be definitive intends to press the point that judgment depends on principles determined, presumably, from standards, and that principles and standards depend on one's idea of tradition. If the kind of writing one likes is just one kind of valuable writing, how does one begin to determine the parameters of value period, not to mention the potency realized out of any "potential" that might emerge as something that should be indelible? For a poem to assume the status of "the indelible" means that behind the art there must be a conception of preeminent value, and not only for one historical moment. It must be translatable from the present relative to the past and into the future. In short, one must have some standard of artistic greatness beyond what is seminal for the time, but potentially elusive (at least at first) to the critical reception of the time as well.

In the mid-19th century pre-dawn of modernism, Matthew Arnold offered a classic vision of tradition—the best that has been said and thought in the world. Though Arnold's own range of inclusion was rather narrower than what the 20th and 21st centuries have pressed upon us, his pithy summation offers an ideal that implies the most acute kind of judgment for selection as well as for exclusion. A century later, after two world wars and the radical redefinitions of modernist practice, Auden questioned Arnold's concept of tradition, declaring simply: "Arnold's notion of Touchstones by which to measure all poems always struck me as a doubtful one, like to turn readers into snobs and ruin talented poets by tempting them to imitate what is beyond their powers."[21] By contrast, Auden summarily shifts the emphasis away from any talk of Touchstones. Tradition, he counters, is "no longer a means of working handed down from generation to generation to the next; a sense of tradition now means the whole of the past as present, yet at the same time as a structured whole the parts of which are related to the terms of before and after."[22] Originality no longer means working to develop "a slight modification of style," but rather to discover "one's authentic voice." Nonetheless, for Auden, good taste meant one was "compelled to exclude,"[23] which implies that authenticity and originality can often fail to produce work of lasting value.

Writing at about the same time as Auden, Randall Jarrell rhapsodized "there is surely some order of the world, some level of being . . . in which the lost plays of Aeschylus are no different from those that have been preserved, an order in which the past, the present, and the future have in some sense the same reality."[24] Here we find a version of tradition as a kind of secular City of God, which allows Jarrell to affirm a vast continuity from the labor of making to the order of being through which, with which, and in which such labors find their purpose and meaning: "The poet writes his poem for his own sake, for the sake of that order of things in which the poem takes the place that has awaited it."[25] Jarrell's vision of tradition as composing "the order of things" in which the poem takes its appropriate place is astonishingly inclusive, containing works lost to time, or lost works by already recognized writers rather than works by the unknown great—if the latter can even be conceived of as a category. Selection and exclusion at this "level of being" become irrelevant—even the lost win entry, at least if your work is as good as Aeschylus's lost plays: though the net appears wider than that, including "the poet" in some representative sense. Or was Jarrell's effusion just an ecstatic moment of unbridled faith, if not in God then in some order of the world above the world? Only a few pages earlier Jarrell takes a different tack: "People realize that almost all fiction or poetry is bad or mediocre—it is the nature of things."[26] He believes the same is true of criticism.

Jarrell's double vision with respect to tradition starkly juxtaposes the utmost idealism with an unwavering reality principle. If the ideal were true, "tradition" at Jarrell's most encompassing level of being would imply something like universal salvation on the order of Origen or Gregory of Nyssa, where in the fullness of time there is nothing that is not saved, not even the incalculable loss of Sappho's poetry, much less the lost plays of Aeschylus— all the lost great preserved in a kind of trans-Platonic state of ever-accruing literary bliss. Conversely, for all of his conservatism, T.S. Eliot's ideas about tradition strike a balance between two extremes, let's call them the empyrean and the empirical views. It is a balance many continue to be unwilling to recognize. For Eliot, tradition should not involve a "blind or timid adherence" to the work of previous generations.[27] Rather, a poet's active engagement with tradition requires "great labour," and involves among other commitments the poet's pursuit of "the historical sense . . . a perception, not only of the pastness of the past, but of its presence." The historical sense, in turn, requires the poet to "write not merely with his own generation in his bones, but with a feeling that the whole of the literature of Europe from Homer and within the whole of the literature of his own country has a simultaneous existence and composes a simultaneous order."[28] In short, Eliot's version of tradition holds "the timeless and the temporal together." Belatedly in his essay "The Literary Dictator," American poet Michael Ryan declares Eliot's views on the subject of tradition "absurdly idealized," to which one might add Eliot's Eurocentrism, not to mention his rather unsavory views about ethnicity and race. Long before Ryan, Auden in *The Dyer's Hand* took issue with Eliot's claim that tradition must be acquired "at great labour." It is this claim, Auden believes, that betrays Eliot as something other than a European critic—only an American could claim such a thing, and indeed Eliot labored to be European as much as he labored to be traditional. So much for Eliot's ideal order, in Auden's estimation.

Yet, for all of its idealism, for all of its interfusion of pseudo-Platonic, timeless "existing monuments" with an Aristotelian ever-evolving temporal reality of poets aspiring to make great poems, Eliot's view of tradition is in fact anything but static. "What happens when a new work of art is created is something that happens simultaneously to all the works of art that preceded it," he reflects, such that "while the existing monuments form an ideal order among themselves," the ideal order of tradition "is modified by the new (the really new) work of art among them."[29] Eliot's notion of tradition requires both integral *completion* from the standpoint of its having an undeniable past, and inherent *alteration*, for without novelty tradition atrophies. A genuinely new work alters the past by re-ordering our consciousness of the past and thereby repositioning both the present order and the potential order of the future. While it might well be impossible for a poet to retain consciously everything ever written within the limited scope of Europe, or merely within the English language, still, to hold up the ideal that requires a poet to pursue "the historical sense" should strike one as a necessity for seriousness in the art. If nothing else, the historical sense is a necessary means for poets to enlarge their capacities of mind and feeling, and to develop and enlarge the practice of the art. If we expand Eliot's cultural and historical frame of reference beyond the compelling but perhaps overly comfortable niche of Europe to allow for other influences, other novel admixtures, translations, underrepresented voices, then the idea of tradition that Eliot articulated nearly one hundred years ago begins to approach a concept capacious enough for our own historical moment. The dynamic order that is tradition widens scope. Tradition is emergent. It reconfigures from a local history to a global one. Such a view places Eliot's belief that "no poet, no artist, has his [or her] complete meaning alone" in an entirely more inclusive context.

This expanded relevance of tradition, should one seek to negotiate the fraught continuum between extremes—what and who belongs in "the Hall" and who and what falls away—requires a further consideration of terms. Tradition, from the Latin *tradere*, "to hand over," and canon, from the Greek *kanon, kana*, or "cane" are not entirely the same thing and emphasize somewhat different processes, or perhaps different aspects of one process. One can "hand over" anything one deems valuable for any variety of reasons, sentimental or otherwise. Canon, however, declares that what is handed over must ultimately "measure up" to the mark already established by what came before. The establishment of religious canons through deliberations over sacred texts that have taken hundreds of years trace a process of selection often far more contentious than blithely deliberative where flesh, blood, and presumably souls hung in the balance, not only texts. Eliot tends to conflate tradition and canon, the dynamics of "handing over" and the dynamics of "measuring up." While the poet's mind must take account of existing monuments to attain a place in the ideal order, that same mind, infused with the historical sense, must likewise "abandon nothing en route."[30] From the anthologist's standpoint, one might choose a poem for inclusion that indeed has significant value from a strictly historical vantage, though it may not "measure up" aesthetically.

Consider again the photograph in the Gotham Book Mart with its notables and greats seated together. From a purist's perspective, we should not confuse the merely notable with the truly great. On the other hand, another editor might incline more broadly such that excellent choices inevitably belie the imperative to "hand over" in the larger sense, thereby allowing space for more poets, additional voices. The second approach, call it the historicist, advances a conception of tradition without sufficient account for the measuring function of canon formation, while the first must guard against reifying the established past. The first approach inclines to the reactive currency of the time capsule; the second the mustiness of the archive.

Navigating these extremes in her prescient essay "Owning the Masters," Marilyn Nelson recognizes that poets like herself, Paul Lawrence Dunbar, Claude McKay, Langston Hughes, Robert Hayden, and Gwendolyn Brooks—among many—also are "heirs of an alternative tradition, heirs of slave narratives, spirituals, great orators, jazz and blues."[31] Still, she vigorously asserts, "the once enslaved are the heirs of the masters, too." Nelson, in turn, affirms the rightness of this idea of tradition, and finds her view resonant with T.S. Eliot's "Tradition and the Individual Talent." "Too often," she muses, "we ignore the fact that tradition is process" and is "formed as we go forward."[32] In short, Nelson endorses Eliot's idea of tradition as dynamic rather than merely retrospective. That endorsement resides emphatically in the demand she places on overcoming "time-bound limitations" such as the legacy of oppression through the very same labors by which one seeks to obtain tradition. Nelson goes further. "I'm convinced," she affirms, that "our inclination to create race-, gender- and ethnic specific enclaves is dangerous," for that tendency disinvites us "from community." Owning the masters in every sense ultimately gives us a way instead "to escape the merely personal, puts us in dialogue with the great thoughts of the past, and teaches us transparency."[33] In Marilyn Nelson's enlarged understanding of Eliot's concept of tradition, poets are called at once to become heirs of a wider set of historical and cultural inheritances and to measure up to what is unequivocally great. Likewise, the late Kashmiri-American poet Agha Shahid Ali qualifies Auden's earlier critique of Matthew Arnold when he reflects: "If Matthew Arnold's touchstones exclude wonderful women writers let's include them by all means. But let's not throw out the best in a service to correct past wrongs. We must enlarge our sympathies, historicize simplicities and complexities, and learn even from—dare I say it—fascists such as Pound, Wyndham Lewis, and Eliot."[34] Marilyn Nelson it appears would agree.

Not so, Kazim Ali. Kazim Ali, like Shahid Ali, is a Muslim American poet who in an open letter to fellow poet Aimee Nezhukumatathil declared with imposing certainty: "The notion of an unbiased concept of literary merit is an inherently and inescapably racist principle. An institution that relies on it is by definition a white supremacist institution."[35] Granting, as Shahid Ali does, all of the brutally exploitative biases of history, Kazim Ali's declaration sounds prejudicial, emphatically so. Is the idea of literary merit inherently "white supremacist," or merely so when it claims to be utterly objective and therefore unbiased? Or does the existence of bias in determining of literary merit render the category something worse than useless? This is exactly what Adrienne Rich implied in her curated edition of *Best American Poetry 1996*, a decision for which Kazim Ali expresses deep sympathy (a poem of his, by his own admission, appeared in that volume).[36] If so, is not the appellation "the best" the most self-evident of misnomers? What does the disappearance of literary merit as an aesthetic category mean for any culture, including "non-white" cultures— think of Basho in Japan, Li Bai in China, Ghalib in the Urdu language, Soyinka in Africa. Acknowledging the inevitable limitations and biases of histories and cultures, do we simply forego the honest quest for aesthetic excellence with an assurance that transcends political currency? Should not marginalized voices be celebrated inclusively with models of authentic literary excellence (drawn from across many cultural inheritances) and not merely with models of inclusivity which, in Kazim Ali's case, elide aesthetic judgments?

Some twenty-five years ago in his essay "American Poetry and American Life," Robert Pinsky implicitly addressed the conflict between the purist and the historicist, the meritorious and the marginalized in a manner that foreshadowed Nelson's instructive negotiation of the conflict's basic terms. "If the truest political component of poetry," Pinsky wrote, "is the sense of whom the poem belongs to—the sense of what social manners, assumptions and tastes the poem imagines—modern American poetry has been uniquely situated, between the old, aristocratic authority of the form and against that authority a powerful, shifting social reality."[37] What lies beneath both the aristocracy of tradition's reliably adaptive integrity of form and order, and a shifting social reality that prizes the relative over the ideal, with the consequent demurral over questions of hierarchy, is the radical skeptic's creed that any attempt at valuation is at best arbitrary, and at worst a covert exercise in power. Contrary to both, Marilyn Nelson asks simply but powerfully: "How can a poet survive without tradition?" To measure one's work only against one's contemporaries "in the pages of the latest issues of one or two literary journals, instead of against the old masters of our tradition" is to indulge in a profound impoverishment of the richer literary community that we are and would become. At the same time, one can see how poets like Audre Lorde would prefer to "disown" the masters given the trauma of slavery. Lorde embraces Nelson's "alternative tradition" of slave narratives and spirituals, orators, jazz and blues, and feels no need to move outside its boundaries, and for perfectly understandable political reasons. Like Nelson, on the other hand, one can understand how disowning the masters might just narrow artistic expression and curtail the hopes of a more inclusive order of community, of a more inclusive tradition.

To cordon off that "alternative tradition" would certainly impoverish the tradition of poetry in the English language. Practically speaking, one can look at an iconic poem like Langston Hughes' "The Weary Blues," composed more or less contemporaneously with the publication of T.S. Eliot's "The Wasteland" and Wallace Stevens's *Harmonium,* to see how a master poet works inclusively across boundaries to enlarge the scope of tradition. Hughes's poem draws from "the long tradition of oral performance and musical improvisation"[38] as well as the social and cultural nexus from which the blues form springs, though it also incorporates constituent forms from the mainline of European and American poetry. Here is the opening:

> Droning a drowsy syncopated tune,
> Rocking back and forth to a mellow croon,
>   I heard a Negro play.
> Down on Lenox Avenue the other night
> By the pale dull pallor of an old gas light
>   He did a lazy sway . . .
>   He did a lazy sway . . .
> To the tune o' those Weary Blues.
> With his ebony hands on each ivory key
> He made that poor piano moan with melody.
>   O Blues!
> Swaying to and fro on his rickety stool
> He played that sad raggy tune like a musical fool.
>   Sweet Blues!
> Coming from a black man's soul.[39]

Hughes's great poem incorporates masterfully the musical and vocal attributes of the tradition of blues singing onto the page, using as Robert Patterson reflects "repetition as a means of gaining time to improvise a response to a life situation."[40] Hughes employs rhyme, some slant rhyme, and intermixes what might be understood to be a call and response modulation between the "written" portions of the poem and the "spoken" lines enclosed in quotations at the end of the first and the beginning of the second stanzas. Those "spoken" or "sung" indented lines constitute the purest adaptation of the blues form into the poem. They form its heart.

At the same time, the poem's opening lines and especially its final five lines exhibit a masterful incorporation of rhymed couplets and tercets, both self-evidently well-tooled formal attributes of the English tradition: "The singer stopped playing and went to bed / While the Weary Blues echoed through his head. / He slept like a rock or a man that's dead." What we discover in Hughes's poem, with even a cursory look, is the commingling of Nelson's "alternative tradition" with the tradition "owned" by the masters. Hughes accomplishes his "owning of the masters" through the poem's formal accomplishment line to line and in the shape of the whole. From this standpoint, "The Weary Blues" is a true hybrid, a remarkable embodiment of tradition vitally modulated from inside and outside simultaneously. If that were not enough, like all blues, Hughes's poem aims at transcendence. As Ralph Ellison underscores in *Shadow and Act*, at the heart of the blues resides "an impulse to keep the painful details and episodes of a brutal experience alive in one's aching consciousness, to finger its jagged grain, and to transcend it, not by consolation of philosophy but by squeezing from it a near-tragic, near comic lyricism."[41] Surely it would be an impoverishment for the Western tradition not to embrace those heirs of any alternative tradition who measure up artistically. Contrarily, to claim the concept "literary merit" is, at best, beside the point does a terrible disservice to Hughes's poetry.

How does a poet's work come to measure up artistically, acknowledging of course the multiple traditions within the larger stream of what gets handed over, and all aiming ideally to measure up? In his essay "A Darkly Defense of Dead White Males," Agha Shahid Ali offers an elegantly nuanced, implicit response to this question when he distinguishes between subject matter and content. For Ali, subject matter "is artistically interesting only when through form it has become content . . . . The more rigorous the form, realized formally, openly, or brokenly, the greater the chance for content."[42] For Shahid Ali, content is more than subject matter, information. It is what happens when the poem's materials have become indelibly transfigured into the artfulness of the poem. As such, for Shahid Ali, it is the pressurizing effect of form, realized variously, that represents the common attribute of "artistic achievement at its highest." The English canonical writers such as Chaucer, Shakespeare, Marlowe, Milton, Donne, and Herbert, and many others share that attribute of intensely realized form, in which language becomes "charged to its utmost." For Ali, neither the traditional "eternals" of subject matter, "birth, death, sex, life, love, loss, grief," nor any political stance liberal or conservative, however culturally, historically, or sociologically valid, can measure up artistically without the alchemizing urgency of form. Ali confesses his own political leanings are distinctly to the Left though, for him, a poem's quality to illuminate the times would not be enough, nor one suspects would some generalized idea of poetic complexity. Not every poem about the Holocaust is compelling nor is every poem about AIDS, Ali states provocatively. Reading Ali's essay, one gains a sense that the politicized category "dead white males" is not a useful way to engage the idea of tradition, nor of canon-making. As a poet who inhabits by his own estimation three cultural traditions simultaneously—Hindu, Muslim, and Western—such shaping historical and cultural inheritances are hugely important for subject matter, but that subject matter inevitably needs to be charged in the poem's formal engagement "at the utmost level" to attain "artistic achievement at its highest." In light of such achievement our response should not be "a hush of reverence," but rather "a great noise in the mind, in the heart."[43]

All this is to say that it is unlikely any poet's work should achieve canonicity based upon subject matter alone. There is, or should remain, a category known as "literary merit" precisely because without such a category all art devolves merely to its subject matter—whether of the "dominant" culture or otherwise. Having taste is not the same thing as having standards, Shahid Ali makes clear, and he presses the point to poets and critics alike with a single, inevitable question: "What are your criteria?" He means the criteria for literary merit, and merit can only be determined in view of what is carried over in a tradition and what measures up. To wit, consider the opening lines of Derek Walcott's "The Schooner Flight":

> In idle August, while the sea soft,
> and leaves of brown islands stick to the rim
> of this Caribbean, I blow out the light
> by the dreamless face of Maria Concepcion
> to ship as a seaman on the schooner *Flight*.
> Out in the yard turning gray in the dawn,
> I stood like a stone and nothing else move
> but the cold sea rippling like galvanize
> and the nail holes of stars in the sky roof,

till a wind start to interfere with the trees.
I pass me dry neighbor sweeping she yard . . . .[44]

Walcott's astonishing command of the mainline tradition of English verse announces itself quintessentially here, the more so since as the passage unfolds Walcott infuses his masterful blank verse ever more extensively and subtly with patois. The blending of tongues begins with the phrase "while the sea soft" to "nothing else move," and continues with the simile "Like galvanize" and again with "sweeping she yard." From here on the dual streams of Walcott's consummate English verse and his patois flow on as a dazzling confluence. This confluence *is* the living tradition. That recognition becomes even more incontestably assured when we realize Walcott has positively appropriated his sonic and formal register from William Langland's "Piers Ploughman":

In a somer seson, whan softe was the sonne,
I shoop me into shroudes as I a sheep were,
In habite as an heremite unholy of werkes,
Wente wide in this world wondres to here.[45]

In short, Walcott's great poem carries forward Langland's visionary masterpiece into another time, another geography, in his postcolonial vision of another Field of Folk. That there are or should be criteria for merit, however contested, should be obvious, and Walcott's poem obviously more than meets the standard. Obvious also should be the recognition that not all works within a tradition are created equal.

Given this simple fact in our time of suspect merit, perhaps it is worth considering briefly the example of Charles Best. Charles Best's "A Sonnet of the Moon" is his sole surviving work. Roughly contemporaneous with Shakespeare, Best was not, alas, the best sonneteer in Queen Elizabeth's time, and this fact becomes clear at the outset of "A Sonnet to the Moon":

Look how the pale queen of the silent night
Doth cause the ocean to attend upon her,

> And he, as long as she is in his sight,
> With her full tide is ready her to honor.[46]

Without attending to every detail in these four lines, one can readily acknowledge a distinct lack of intensity, despite a few metrical substitutions to the prevailing iambic rhythm. Stock phrasing like "silent night" and syntactical inversions like "ready her to honor" do not help to lift the poem off the page, and exert no "great noise in the mind, in the heart." As Best's sonnet proceeds and satisfies the sonnet's formal requirements, the conceit of the feminized moon unfolds through a juxtaposition of opposites—the beloved, like the moon, is high and mounts upward while the lover's "tender heart" remains at low-ebb, or ebbs and flows. Nothing of any great drama finds formal intensity here, nor does it gain in intensity after the volta. Typically, the poem's subject matter is love and longing, and the sonnet remains typical in its treatment of the subject. It moves through its formal requirements with the occasional glimmer of real invention, but never lifts that subject matter through the form, with the form, into some vital content. Best's sonnet keeps its equilibrium without summoning any dramatic tension. Everything in the poem feels received, not transformed, not entirely transfigured out of its subject. Unfairly, one might compare Best's "A Sonnet of the Moon" to Shakespeare's Sonnet 29. Here are the first eight lines before the volta:

> When in disgrace with fortune and men's eyes,
> I all alone beweep my outcast state,
> And trouble deaf Heaven with my bootless cries,
> And look upon myself, and curse my fate,
> Wishing me like to one more rich in hope,
> Featur'd like him, like him with friends possess'd,
> Desiring this man's art, and that man's scope,
> With what I most enjoy contented least . . . .[47]

The most self-evident measure of Shakespeare's genius in Sonnet 29 is his orchestration of the long opening sentence's syntactical movement through the tight formal requirements of the lineation, its meter and rhyme. The octet unfolds dramatically through the long sentence's syntax with a progressive intensifying of emotion and perception. The iambic rhythm carries forward, though Shakespeare modulates that rhythm with trochaic substitutions, as at the head of lines five and six. Then, counterpointing and modulating the sentence's driving motion, the strong medial caesuras in lines four and seven provide a balancing effect. The sestet—really a continuation of the sentence after the colon—accomplishes a true reversal not only of the speaker's emotional state but his spiritual state as well: "Yet in these thoughts myself almost despising . . . ." By the end of the sonnet we have moved with the speaker from lowest lows of social disregard, self-hatred, and despair to "singing hymns at Heaven's gate," such that heaven itself, he realizes through the presence of the beloved, had always been present even in his worst "bootless" feelings and failures.

To compare Best's "A Sonnet of the Moon" with Shakespeare's Sonnet 29 is perhaps indeed a venture in false comparison. Still, it is important to consider from the standpoint of tradition as opposed to canon that there is a place for Best's poem—we fairly regard it through the prism of its literary historical moment. Shakespeare's sonnet is for all time. It has achieved in Ali's sense the measure of language charged to its utmost. To trace forward for a moment the incontestable vibrancy of true merit, one might consider Keats's "Bright Star." Surely it is, if nothing else, a brilliant response to "the call" of Sonnet 29, a call to which Keats's octet bears witness:

> Bright star, would I were steadfast as thou art—
>   Not in lone splendour hung aloft the night
> And watching, with eternal lids apart,
>   Like nature's patient, sleepless Eremite,
> The moving waters at their priestlike task
>   Of pure ablution round earth's human shores,
> Or gazing on the new soft-fallen mask
>   Of snow upon the mountains and the moors—[48]

Like Best's "A Sonnet of the Moon," though unlike Shakespeare's Sonnet 29, Keats's "Bright Star" initially situates us in rarified air—transcendent air. The star is steadfast, lone, its lids eternal, an eremite, a hermit, hung aloft in the poem's metaphysical as well as physical space. As the poem gradually directs our view brilliantly downward, even the waters come to move ritually, baptismally, in their cleansing action. With the dash that signals the end of the octet, Keats's syntax through the lines that follow lowers us further and further into realms of fleshly life, the poet's mind correcting and modulating its judgments along the way. "No—still steadfast, still unchangeable." Keats effortlessly reconfigures our sense of transcendence away from any ethereal spirituality and forces us to acknowledge with him the irrevocable claims of the flesh. Counter to Shakespeare's turn from low to high, Keats brings us from high to low, again in one sweeping sentence. Yet unlike Shakespeare, his mentor in the tradition and the canon, with his final couplet Keats places us in an existential bind: one must live ever in sensual abandon, an immanent embrace of transcendence, or one must "swoon to death." For all its resplendence, by comparison the star is drearily ascetic. Through his intensified engagement with the form of the sonnet, Keats's subject matter—eternity, sex, and death—finally opens a trapdoor into that which lies beyond the binaries of flesh and spirit.

If we fast forward now from Keats's "Bright Star" into the 20th century, we find a further improvisation on tradition through the same resonant theme in a poem considered to be Elizabeth Bishop's last before her own swoon to death. Here is "Sonnet":

> Caught—the bubble
> in the spirit level,
> a creature divided;
> and the compass needle
> wobbling and wavering,
> undecided.
> Freed—the broken
> thermometer's mercury
> running away;
> and the rainbow-bird
> from the narrow bevel
> of the empty mirror,
> flying wherever
> it feels like, gay![49]

From a conservatively formalist vantage, one might say that Bishop's poem is a sonnet in name only, though in fact these mostly fourteen dimeter lines do exactly what should be done, do what "Bright Star" did, only more radically: improvise the form under form's pressure to transfigure the subject into content. Bishop's sonnet turns on the tension of being at once caught and freed. The creature of the poem is divided—is creaturely in every sense. In "Sonnet," consciousness is what divides us, just as what divides us is flesh and spirit in "Bright Star," despair and exaltation in "Sonnet 29," and the ebb and flow of desire unfulfilled in Best's less than accomplished "A Sonnet to the Moon." Here, Bishop's innovative use of form tracks through the brilliant management of her unorthodox rhyme scheme and the rhythms of the poem which, while not prevailingly iambic, nonetheless blaze a path that negotiates equilibrium and disequilibrium both figuratively ("the spirit level") and syntactically ("wobbling and wavering). When liberation comes, we feel with the speaker that we are neither above nor below, nor are we caught in self-indulgent rhapsodies. Instead, flying "wherever" we are freed with the poem into joy.

In "Sonnet," Bishop has transformed subject matter into content through the shaping pressure of form. The same must be said for Shakespeare's Sonnet 29 and Keats's "Bright Star." Though in each case the sonnet provides the template for the poem's formal realization, the form of the poem transcends its structural fulfillment. True form is always a singular manifestation. Form is the transfiguration of subject matter into content made uniquely vital in the work, and never merely the satisfying of an imposed structure, whether assumed at the outset or deferred to by the poet. Poems that embody this vitality of form and content ought to stand a far greater chance of achieving canonicity, leaving aside the trends, prejudices, needs, and whims of literary and cultural history. Indeed, all of these sonnets—Shakespeare's, Keats's, Bishop's—achieve a unique and powerful intensity through the dynamics of opposing directions, conditions, or forces coming to formal embodiment, embodiment that is transfiguring of the conditions but without easy resolution. Together they stand as exemplars of the adaptive power of tradition as well as the need to charge one's art to the uttermost. "Let's face it", as Marianne Boruch bluntly reminds us, "a poem matters because it is about eternal things—death, love, knowledge, time—however these are disguised."[50] Each of these poems, whether explicitly or implicitly, has eternal things on its mind. An awareness of the eternal and the necessary aesthetic pressure it brings to the act of making poems is precisely what is lost when we remove the example of literary merit— standards rather than mere taste—from the writing and appreciation of poetry. And by neglecting or repudiating aesthetics in this way we effectively diminish what might be most worthy of eternal claims in ourselves.

3. *Goodbye Eternity*

In "The Poet and the City" W.H. Auden enumerates several conditions that define the prevailing worldview of the mid-20th century. The first of these is the loss of belief in the eternity of the physical universe. Nature, he reflects, constantly changes, and consequently the modern artist has lost any model of endurance upon which to base the durability of his or her own work. The second is the loss of belief in the reality of sensory phenomena—"modern science," he observes, "has destroyed our faith in the naïve observations of our senses."[51] Third is the loss of belief in a norm of human nature which will always require "some man-fabricated world to be at home in." As such, the artist cannot believe that even the next generation will be able to understand the work of the previous one. Consciousness of the past as present, as Eliot hoped, no longer stands. At best, the "handing down" that is tradition becomes merely an effort of anxiously grasping at the past by the individual artist: it is a species of cupidity, if such access is to be desired at all. Despite Auden's misgivings, some thirty years later Robert Pinsky envisioned tradition "a network of reference and reliance in relation to the past" that reveals its presence in a poem's technique.[52] The future laureate assumes considerable effort has been made by the poet to obtain the kind of knowledge that enables artistic maturation. What he cannot assume, however, is that the nexus of conditions identified by Auden allows for any security in the reception of the poem. This loss of security entails more than the poet's doubt about individual efforts, or understandable concerns over whether that poet will have an audience now or in the future. What I want to underscore is the more pervasive loss of faith in any overarching or "subsumptive" vision of reality (to borrow again from Eliot); that is, the loss of some "level of being" as Jarrell would ideally have it, which would provide a foundation for valuing anything beyond the free-floating plurality in which true literary merit appears baseless. One wants ideally some foundation for measuring aesthetic value with an eye willing to range beyond the transient cultural preferences of the moment, for without that foundation there can be no genuine aesthetic judgment whatsoever. Art becomes merely another species of politics.

The aesthetic insecurity underlining Auden's assessment of the intellectual culture at the middle of the 20th century has its origins in the rise of modernism over several centuries, the gist of which may be understood as a myth of progress, a "meta-narrative" that subsumes all stories into itself—the story of human reason concomitant, paradoxically, with the rise of a wholly materialist cosmos bereft of any spiritual vitality. One sees the vestige of this latter older vision in Jarrell's plea for another level of being. It is relatively easy to see the discord in modern thought between reason bound to no supremely value-establishing dimension and the positivist conclusion that the prima materia of existence is the sole bedrock of all that is. The entryway into postmodernism is a step—really a free fall—into the rupture opened by the modern, self-negating meta-narrative where "truth" is merely the product of the rhetoric of power: "the story" as theologian David Bentley Hart describes it, of "no more stories."[53] In this univocal story, all stories are read through the monocular, "totalizing" lens of their own self-contradiction—the meta-narrative of how narrative is impossible except as parody of its own unmaking. Tradition, however construed, likewise is a variety of meta-narrative about what a culture values, and therefore what a culture values more broadly over the course of its history. There must be novelty in tradition for tradition to exist at all, but tradition also requires continuity. It is this combination of novelty and continuity that has become, it appears at least, unsustainable in view of the metanarrative of radical discontinuity undergirding all we say, and are, and do. This is particularly true of canon formation.

In keeping with this discomfiting vision of things, Czeslaw Milosz envisioned the defining rupture in the western tradition impacting poetry, like everything else, as the gradual replacement of "the vertical orientation," when the human being turned its "eyes toward Heaven," by "a horizontal longing." The horizontal longing, as Milosz calls it, manifests itself once again as a myth of progress that runs hand in hand with an all-consuming nihilism.[54] Needless to say, as a poet living in the merciless crosshairs of 20th-century history, Milosz witnessed the most brutal extremities of unrelenting violence, power, and destruction. "To define in a word what had happened," he reflects, "one can say: disintegration . . . . People always live within a certain order and are unable to visualize when that order might cease to exist."[55] While it would be the height of hyperbole to place the incidental "disintegrations" of tradition in 20th-century poetry on par with Milosz's scale of historical trauma, it would also be delusional to assume poetry has become immune to the loss of Milosz's vertical orientation. It is precisely the loss of the vertical as a sustainable support structure (not to mention supplier of form, content, and the basic terms of our self-understanding) that undermines our reliance on canon-making's faith in evaluative measurement as the guiding light of tradition, *and* our faith in history alone as the contrary litmus. The first depends on an aesthetic elite unsupportable except by the assertion of cultural power, the second on a principle of inclusion almost entirely distinguishable from aesthetic achievement. Either way we end in Nietzsche's dynamic of power.

Pluralism is one thing, relativism another. Recent discussions impacting traditional form have opened a window to just how pervasively relativism rules so many current determinations of value in American poetry. In a world in which "the vertical orientation" has been so devalued, there is now no establishing even taste (much less standards) on any foundation, if only to carry on a genuine disputation. What you like has value for you, which has always been a self-evident assertion. Such claims have the effect of rendering aesthetic value meaningless if left unquestioned. By contrast, when a critical effort to establish some basis for the idea of tradition around legitimate questions of value, practice, and inheritance modulates into a social agenda, as it does in T.S. Eliot's more extreme reflections on culture, the necessary plurality of voices and visions required for any tradition to thrive risks almost inevitable curtailment. Both relativism and nihilism have their philosophical source in nominalism, which has the effect of severing "the perceptible world from the analogical index of divine transcendence."[56] By cutting the cord of meaning across the line of Milosz's vertical axis, we not only lose hope of transcendence but hope for a meaningful world, and hope (as Marilyn Nelson reminds us) of real community and inclusivity. The root of Auden's lament, that we have lost any sense of the eternity of the physical world, likewise finds its central source in this same nominalist rupture. Some thirty years after Auden, Robert Pinsky sheds light on the heart of the matter when he defines nominalism loosely as "the doctrine that words and concepts are mere names, convenient counters of no inherent reality, though they may be useful means for dealing with the atomistic flux of reality."[57] Conversely, realism is "the doctrine of universals" that declares "words and concepts embody reality." From this standpoint, the poet *must* be a realist, however unacknowledged. Otherwise the very act of writing is, on its face, self-contradictory.

Milosz, Auden, and Pinsky affix on the idea of poetry as an embodiment of the real without denying the world's actuality in obvious differences. The world is not composed of one thing, but many. It exists as relation and not merely chaos. So, the world as a composition of differences finds its meaningful orientation only in analogy, for analogy itself is the principle of relation that allows one thing to be "handed over" to another. Analogy is metaphor understood at the level of the macrocosm—the differences between things that mark the deeper connection by which anything comes to be and continues in existence over time. Milosz's idea of poetry as "a passionate pursuit of the real"[58] assumes this analogical perspective, which is the foundation as well of philosophical and theological realism. Though he writes long after the vertical axis has been cut, Wallace Stevens like Milosz affirms essentially the same sense of value when he says poets make "a world that transcends the world and a life livable in that transcendence" because at poetry's root is "a transcendent analogue composed of the particulars of reality, created by the poet's sense of the world."[59] Stevens's secular version of the theologian's "analogical index" is a belated version of the medieval realist's divinely established analogy of being. Where Stevens situates the Archimedean lever at the point of "the poet's sense of the world," theology traditionally establishes its leverage point (that allows the world to be a world, rather than just a compendium of chaotic, nominal disintegrations) in God through whose infinitely generative Being, the being of the world obtains and is sustained.

If one envisions tradition as a concept situated at the midpoint between the microcosm of language and metaphor and the macrocosm of the so-called analogy of being, then tradition's self-defining action of "handing over" operates within the cultural and historical nexus that exists between the individual poet's efforts and the world's embodiment in what necessarily transcends our powers of representation. The world as world is only finitely knowable. When tradition, however, devolves into a nominalist Hall of Mirrors rather than a Hall of Exemplars it loses any capacity to mediate between the imaginative propensities of individual poets and some "supreme fiction" that orients the poet's work—some vision or version of transcendence whether orthodox, heterodox, or merely the post-Romantic doctrine of imagination as necessary angel. This loss of "true north" is debilitating to poetry. "What artist would not establish himself there where the organized center of all movement in time and space—which he calls the mind or heart of creation—determines every function?" So Stevens believed with Paul Klee.[60] Stevens goes so far as to invoke the philosopher, social advocate, and mystic Simone Weil to give final credence to his judgment that "modern reality is a reality of decreation, in which our revelations are not the revelations of belief, but the precious portents of our own powers." Milosz likewise invokes Weil as a chastening exemplar for poets who, failing to sense "the vital center," have become so "enmeshed in professional rituals" they become "ashamed" of "discriminating between values."[62]

If anything characterizes contemporary poetry, it is surely the lack of a vital center. Not surprisingly, in lieu of that center, all kinds of professional rituals and preferences fill the void. Perhaps it would be better to say that there are vital *centers* in 21st-century poetry. The plethora of stylistic approaches is not at issue. Cause for concern, however, is arbitrariness of what rises to the fore, given the fortunes of access in what has become a heavily professionalized endeavor: The Poetry Business. One could choose from hundreds if not thousands of poems that place a premium on the currency of superficial regard. Of these, Dorothea Lasky's "Ars Poetica" will serve well to illustrate the kind of work that seems more and more to be of the moment. Here is how the poem opens:

> I wanted to tell the veterinary assistant about the cat video Jason
> sent me
> But I resisted for fear she'd think it strange
> I am very lonely
> Yesterday my boyfriend called me, drunk again
> And interspersed between ringing tears and clinginess
> He screamed at me with a kind of bitterness
> No other human had before to my ears
> And told me that I was no good
> Well maybe he didn't mean that
> But that is what I heard
> When he told me my life was not worthwhile
> And my life's work the work of the elite.[63]

Lasky's poem begins with a rambling non-sequitur that, one suspects, is perfectly faithful to the documentary truth of what happened, what Richard Hugo called the triggering subject of a poem—the incipient node of energy from which it needs to depart in order to obtain any hope at lasting value. Lasky's poem takes up all the stridency and melodrama of adolescent hurt, but never establishes the necessary aesthetic distance from its subject matter. One sees many like tones when one teaches undergraduate poetry workshops, though Lasky is the author of at least three duly noted books of poems, and "Ars Poetica" may be found on the website of The Poetry Foundation, home to the legendary *Poetry* magazine. Underneath the surface chattiness and formal sketchiness of Lasky's poem, nothing much of consequence surfaces. The shallows only become shallower as the poem continues:

> I say I want to save the world but really
> I want to write poems all day
> I want to rise, write poems, go to sleep,
> Write poems in my sleep
> Make my dreams poems
> Make my body a poem with beautiful clothes
> I want my face to be a poem
> I have just learned how to apply

> Eyeliner to the corners of my eyes to make them appear wide
> There is a romantic abandon in me always

The wideness of the speaker's eyes is what it appears to be—merely decorative, entirely unfazed by "the dread of others" to which the poem gives nod in the lines that follow. The poem lacks any real engagement with the world beyond the poet's own overweening desire to be a poet, to be regarded in that professional capacity, that singular "good." One fears her boyfriend may be right, that she may be no good in every sense, though perhaps this last speculation is cruel. Then again, as Lasky declares near the poem's end, "goodness is beside the point." The only point in Lasky's final analysis is "holding onto things." We do not know what things those would be, perhaps her boyfriend or Jason—are they the same person? The poem is unclear on the matter, perhaps beautiful things—but goodness has already been shucked free of beauty, beauty scoured of goodness, scoured away along with the things of the world. There is, by the poet's limited sightlines, an unbridgeable gap between the unsaved world and whatever the poet claims to hold onto. By the end of Lasky's poem nothing is held or beheld, only the poem as self-serving object. What we have is the professionally made poem. Lasky's self-regarding romantic abandon in "Ars Poetica" abandons the world, goodness, and, finally, any valorizing idea of beauty for the poet's art, or tradition—what we should hold onto in every sense for the sake of the past and for the future. Lasky's poem is not an example of art for art's sake, but of art for the poet's sake.

The tendency to become involved in "professional rituals" was never a challenge for Simone Weil, that exemplar so important to Stevens and Milosz. From early in her life, Weil exemplified a passionate commitment to the poor and working classes, despite having been born into a Jewish family of free thinkers—an economic and intellectual elite. Her father was a doctor and her brother, Andre, Weil one of the great mathematicians of the 20th century. Her own passions turned toward philosophy, and literature, and, eventually, Christian mysticism and the Vedas. She made her living as a schoolteacher, though her work as labor organizer was just as significant. Her desire to share fully in the life of the working classes led her to seek work in various factories under arduous conditions despite a physical constitution ill-equipped for such labor. Called a communist and an anarchist, she argued with party leaders including Trotsky about the fate of Europe, renounced her pacifism with the rise of Hitler, fought alongside republicans in the Spanish Civil War, and found herself experiencing to her own chagrin what can only be called mystical states, the first upon encountering the crucifix at the Basilica of Santa Clara in Assisi. For years, in sympathy with the lowest classes of society, and eventually with those starving under German occupation, she ate only minimally, and died in 1943 in England at the age of thirty-four, still with plans to parachute into occupied France. Today she would be regarded as anorexic, though beyond any psychological issues her curtailment of food had both a foundation in social justice and in her theological reflections. Her parents and her brother had already immigrated to the United States from Nazi-occupied France during the last months of her life. Weil refused any safe haven and sought to join the Resistance despite suffering from tuberculosis and the physical frailty that would kill her. It is almost unaccountable that her mostly posthumous writings influenced 20th-century poets as widely unalike politically and aesthetically as T.S. Eliot, Wallace Stevens, and Czeslaw Milosz.

Simone Weil's importance as a philosopher and a religious, social, and literary thinker is as unlikely as it is incalculable. That importance endures into our postmodern time. Anne Carson pays a kind of homage to Weil's significance (if not her vision) in the poetic pseudo-opera, "Decreation." In Carson's work, "Chocolate Dancers" whirl about the stage, among other absurdities. Emphatically postmodernist, Carson's work strains to gain aesthetic credibility either as opera or as poetry, though the "Decreation Aria" sung by a fictionalized Weil captures something of the extremity and urgency of the thinker's understanding of the relationship between God, creation, and decreation:

> I am excess.
>> Flesh.
>> Brain.
>> Breath.

> Creature who
> breaks the silence of heaven,
> blocks God's view of his beloved creation
> and like an unwelcome third between two lovers
> gets in the way.[64]

Weil's starkly apophatic, almost world-denying understanding of Creator and creation finds stark articulation in these lines—it is a view that led Eliot to see her as a belated Cathar, a modern-day follower of the Gnostic thinker Marcion, given her less than sympathetic view of the God of the Hebrew Bible. She regarded the Hebrew God a national deity, autocratic, and therefore not the monotheistic, Hellenized God of the Judeo-Christian tradition, which she effectively embraced in her radically unorthodox way. Her circumspection towards the God of Israel constitutes the most controversial aspect of her thought, though it must be said that she likewise had serious objections to the Catholic Church. She held that, as an institution, the Church continued to advance, however unintentionally, the materialist oppression of ancient Rome from which it secured its universal claims. Ultimately it was the social structure of the Church she feared, the allure of a collectivity that made it a terrestrial body, and therefore bound it to "the Prince of this World."[65] Conversely, as she wrote to her spiritual confidant Father Perrin, her knowledge of "Greece, Egypt, ancient India and ancient China, the beauty of the world, the pure and authentic reflections of this beauty in art and mathematics," and what she had seen "of the inner recesses of the human heart where religious belief is unknown," all did as much she claimed "as the visibly Christian ones" to deliver her "into Christ's hands . . . even more." It was these exemplary realities, "outside visible Christianity," that prevented her from joining the Church: "The children of God should not have any other country here below but the universe itself."[66] She affirmed this conviction, remaining unbaptized to her death. She also affirmed unsparingly that everything in the universe, not least of which human beings, had been thrown into the material conditions of necessity and chance—thrown here into affliction not by any intermediary pseudo-deity but by none other than God.

To say Weil was ethically uncompromising would be an understatement. Her theological ideas are no less extreme—hers is an ardently negative theology. At the same time, Weil's vision is not nihilistic—the extremity of her view of life as provisional heightens her commitment to the Creator as the source of compassion for others as well as for the world. Despite the all -too -human tendency to interpose, often brutally, between the uncreated and the created, Weil recognizes that it is only by virtue of the uncreated that the created world has any value whatsoever. It is for this reason that she stood so strongly against the culture of her own moment, preferring the ancient Greeks, the medieval mystics, the Vedas. So where in our time Carson portrays Weil as an almost comically self-indulgent figure, we find Milosz worrying two decades earlier that such views as Weil's and his own might well be labeled reactionary. Yes, they might, and maybe even more so now than when they were initially made. Just so, Carson's genre-bending text runs the risk of tapering Weil's principle of decreation to a mere psychological disorder rather than what it is: a vision of reality resonant with theological and spiritual urgency running through and across multiple traditions, East and West. In keeping with this accurate accounting, the idea of tradition itself expresses the deep human need for what Weil called "rootedness." "To be rooted," she believed, "is perhaps the most important and least recognized need of the human soul."[67] Yet the experience of "uprootedness" so characterizes both her time and ours. "A human being has roots," she declares, "by virtue of his real, active, and natural participation in the life of a community which preserves in living shape certain particular treasures of the past and certain particular expectations for the future."[68] Tradition is precisely that living shape, at once preserving and evolving. With the loss of eternity, and with the loss of rootedness even of the claims of meaning, what does Weil's concept of decreation have to teach us about how we might regard tradition and the highest aspirations of individual poems?

4. *The Closed Door, the Way Through*

That poets as widely different in temperament as Wallace Stevens and Czeslaw Milosz invoke for their art the thought and example of a brilliant Jewish French political, social, and secular religious philosopher who embraced Catholic spirituality but who refused baptism and arguably died through complications of self-inflicted starvation at the very nadir of the Second World War is surprising, if not remarkable. Anne Carson's recent fascination underscores the durability of Weil's vision for our historical and cultural moment, as does Edward Hirsch's poems "Simone Weil: The Year of Factory Work" and "Away from Dogma," as well as the book-length poem, *The Red Virgin*, by Stephanie Strickland.

The concept of decreation is central to Weil's thought and, incongruously enough, central to Stevens's and Milosz's reflections on their art. If destruction is "to make something created pass into nothingness," then decreation to the contrary is "to make something created pass into the uncreated."[69] For Weil the whole purpose of life is "to undo the creature in us," to make passage against or, better, through the "deifugal" force of creation moving outward from God into the uncreated, which she affirms is God's own life. "We participate in the creation of the world by decreating ourselves," Weil believes, which from her perspective involves the utmost in renunciation: "We must become nothing, we must go down to the vegetative level; it is then that God becomes bread."[70] The ego is nothing. The true "I" is hidden and lives "on the side of God." Imagination, far from being Coleridge's shaping power—"a repetition in the finite mind of the Eternal Act of creation in the Infinite I Am"—is precisely the power that prevents humanity from "seeing how much the essence of the necessary differs from that of the good."[71] For Weil imagination blinds us to what is really real; it does not in the least constitute a reflection of the image of God's creative power. Rather it weaves a veil, it exemplifies our "degradation."[72] There is an almost dire radicalism to this way of thinking, a very near world-denying inclination that verges beyond the nominalist into the nihilist, the masochistic. How could Weil's vision provide an affirming flame even for religiously inclined poets, much less poets seeking to make the most of their own powers without appeal to religious ideas of order?

For one thing, creation and decreation are part and parcel of each other—the created requires decreation, the answering counter movement: "The world is the closed door. It is the barrier. And at the same time, it is the way through."[73] How so? Despite imagination's tendency to blind us, the barrier is the way through because the created world is the middle ground, metaxu, a bridge composed of bridges, a zone of similarity-in-difference that exists as such to carry us over from the created to the uncreated. For Weil, God's *kenosis* or self-emptying simultaneously permits creation to exist and constitutes God's withdrawal from that creation. We are left with "the essence of created things as intermediaries."[74] The role of the poet, then, in Weil's view, is to look beyond the limits of imagination into what she regards as the true subject of art. That true subject, the core content to be embodied in form, is "sensible and contingent beauty discerned through the network of chance and evil."[75] Wallace Stevens essentially places the theological force of decreation in brackets. He aestheticizes the idea. For Stevens, the term decreation speaks to modern poetry's tendency to re-imagine the real the way Cézanne sees abstract lines and planes and represents them in newly formed configurations. Like Weil, however, Stevens had a strong affinity with Plato, which might explain the tendency toward abstraction in both. Milosz, to further complicate things, sees Weil's thought as a practical countermeasure against wanton destruction and, therefore, a counterforce akin to Stevens's idea of "the violence within" exerting itself against "the violence without." It is this violence that sustains the poet's consciousness, confronted as it is by disintegration. Like Weil's, Milosz's temperament demands reverence for the past, since it is through the distance of time that we are enabled "to see reality without coloring it with our passions."[76] In his own way Milosz embraces the theological reach of Weil's idea. Where Weil's decreation enables a poet like Stevens to see art as a transcendent analogy such that the created thing, the poem, approximates the uncreated, decreation empowers Milosz to value "the passionate pursuit of the real" through intermediaries, bridges, metaxu. In just this way, on the larger scale of history and culture, tradition hands itself over to the poet who loves it, for on one hand it binds the poet's work to the past, while on the other it pitches the work forward to the future through the poet's encounter with reality.

From this double perspective, Weil's decreation conjoins a penchant for invention and novelty with reverence and continuity. Or, from Auden's perspective, if "the poet's activity in creating a poem is analogous to God's activity," then every poem "is an attempt to present an analogy to that paradisal state in which Freedom and Law, System and Order are united in harmony."[77] The great work of art is the created so concentrated in its making it is as if it had entered into the perfected life of the uncreated through the conditions of necessity, chance, and evil. Great poems decreate the world through the world's very worldliness, as well as the worldliness of the poem into a promise of the uncreated. Art is a promise of that perfection, an attempt "to transport into a limited quantity of matter . . . an image of the infinite beauty of the entire universe."[78] In this manner, art is analogous to virtue, in that both are the products of extreme attention, attention that is itself analogous to prayer.[79]

I want to look now at a few poems that not only achieve this degree of artistic perfection, but do so by dramatizing the decreative experience itself insofar as it is possible to imagine what is finally unimaginable. Emily Dickinson's "I felt a Funeral, in my Brain," imagines the unimaginable, remarkably enough, with vivid immediacy. Throughout Dickinson's poem we track the speaker's consciousness inside the theater of the mind, and the mind watching itself comes to the brink of its own passage beyond existence itself. First the Mourners appear—are they thoughts treading to and fro, trying to make sense of what lies beyond the senseless? Then the drumbeat of the service begins, at which point the mind itself numbs and the box lifts, and the Soul hears itself creak across itself while all of Space begins to toll. In the poem's final two stanzas, Dickinson brings the reader to the very limit of knowing—to what Weil would have regarded as the threshold between the created and the uncreated:

> As all the Heavens were a Bell,
> And Being but an Ear,
> And I and Silence, some strange Race
> Wrecked, solitary, here—
>
> And then a Plank in Reason, broke,
> And I dropped down, and down—
> And hit a World, at every plunge,
> And Finished knowing—then—[80]

C.K. Williams believes that Dickinson's poem enacts "the terrifying closed system of depression."[81] The poem certainly can be read that way. Yet, where Dickinson's poem brings us is somewhere out beyond depression's admittedly devastating emotional trauma. We are on the final bridge, the ultimate metaxu, its brink, the place where being carries itself across and is handed over into un-being, or being beyond our human capacity to know. That bridge, because it must, caves open. There, with the "I," worlds plunge into unknowing—the ontological, the epistemological underpinnings of physical life and consciousness, like London's bridges in the old children's rhyme, all fall down. Yet, remarkably, Dickinson renders this impossible state beyond states in the past tense—it happened "then." Is Dickinson's poem a brilliant enactment of the moment of death's annihilating power, the poet's projection into the past of what is sure to come inevitably in the future? It is that. Though Dickinson's poem captures also Weil's conception of death as "an instantaneous state, without past or future . . . Indispensable for entering into eternity."[82] The poem's final extraordinary fiction is that the "I" speaks out of its post-created life beyond all knowing back into the ear of being, to tell the human listener what happened before time ceased for the soul.

Dickinson is at her most extraordinary when her poems speak of the paradoxically condition-less condition of some posthumous life, the life of the uncreated. Her "I heard a fly buzz—when I died" marks a similar enactment. The interposition of the fly just before the windows fail and the speaker can no longer "see to see" creates a pause that allows the light to linger just brightly enough before all converges into the onset of what lies beyond all seeing: *kataphasis*, the visionary, erupts into *apophasis*, what lies beyond knowing. Here, again, the poem acts as bridge, as metaphor that carries us over if not into the uncreated then to its liminal analogy in the theater of consciousness itself. Similarly, in "Because I could not stop for death" Dickinson ventures to bring us beyond the threshold of the created into the uncreated, or at least to figure death as something other than instantaneous and therefore un-representable. In the poem, Death is a suitor, the post-creaturely "life" a journey that takes one past familiar places, and the fiction of the uncreated is given physical credence in a sudden disruptive reversal of motion:

> We passed the School, where Children strove
> At Recess—in the Ring—
> We passed the Fields of Gazing Grain—
> We passed the Setting Sun—
>
> Or rather—He passed us—[83]

In this version of the afterlife as journey, the physical reality of time's relative motion becomes a figure for the metaphysical passage of departing, almost leisurely, outside created life. Dickinson's image reads like an Einstein thought experiment. At poem's end centuries pass, though they pass in hardly a day. In death, the horses' heads are "toward eternity," as though Dickinson had glimpsed a vision of the eternal as some infinitely decelerating motion—Zeno's arrow perpetually moving in space as it advances eternally by halves toward its target: being as act stretching outward in relation rather than toward some static final point.

"Toward eternity" suggests a version of the uncreated as somehow bound together with movement, a kind of eschatology that appears to be more an unfolding, even in the afterlife, rather than a seismic transformation into an unimaginable Otherness. In Dickinson's "Because I could not stop for death" we have what might be called an aesthetic eschatology, since the passage beyond death into the uncreated is figurative, that is, analogical. By the end of the poem the uncreated is "fleshed out" in the soul's journey. I want to pursue further the idea of poems "fleshing out" the uncreated by stopping for a moment at two other very great poems: W.B. Yeats's "Sailing to Byzantium" and Wallace Stevens's "Of Mere Being." The first stanza of "Sailing to Byzantium" establishes the relationship between the created and the uncreated in starkest contrast:

> That is no country for old men. The young
> In one another's arms, birds in the trees—
> Those dying generations—at their song,
> The salmon-falls, the mackerel-crowded seas,
> Fish, flesh, or fowl, commend all summer long
> Whatever is begotten, born, and dies.
> Caught in that sensual music all neglect

Monuments of unageing intellect.[84]

Underscored by the "sensual music" of the alliterative "f" sounds through lines four and five, Yeats's dying generations exist in culpable relief of the "monuments of unageing intellect." Here we see how Yeats's view of art advances an idea of tradition that dovetails with canon in a narrow gate of admittance—only monuments of unageing intellect can teach the poet how to sing, despite the poem's simultaneous acknowledgment that all neglect them. Yeats's assertion affirms what is in essence a paradox. The poem's embrace of the monumental, its appeal to the singing school of tradition, finds formal integrity in his adaptation of ottava rima, the stanza pattern Byron used in "Don Juan" to carry the reader along on his rollicking tale of one life out of all the dying generations. Yeats's formal choice exists in counterpoint to the poem's sensual music, but beyond this brilliantly dynamic fusion of aesthetic opposites, his choice to reconfigure Byron's form for a poem more akin to a four-part Byzantine frieze than a narrative romp demonstrates how tradition— even of the monumental variety—is anything but a static reception of the past without reinvention.

In the two stanzas that follow, Yeats heightens the contrast between the "paltry thing" of his own life, that dying animal, and the artifices of eternity that permit entry into the uncreated as figured in Byzantium. "Studying / monuments of its own magnificence" is how one books passage to the uncreated—a more heroic journey in Yeats than we find in Dickinson's leisurely coach ride. Having departed created nature, in one of the great and strangest figures in poetry, Yeats transfigures himself from the aged man he is into a golden bird, a figure for the utterly unnatural, the wholly denatured work of art that, by being outside nature, paradoxically sees—"what is past or passing or to come." Now, the poet, transmogrified, can see all time in its entirety, and thus comes to share (despite his heterodoxy) in something of the divine "Eternal Now" as St. Augustine called it. In "Sailing to Byzantium" the measure of all art is the distance the artist has been able to travel beyond created being into the uncreated, or as if. Though Yeats never expressly calls poetry an art of decreation, his vision is entirely decreative, though with the one caveat that like

Dickinson he ventures giving us a vision of the uncreated in a figurative rather than a historical Byzantium.

In contrast to "Sailing to Byzantium," "Of Mere Being" offers a vigorously stringent vision of the uncreated, though perhaps not as stringent as Dickinson's in "I felt a funeral in my brain" or "I heard a fly buzz when I died." Both of Dickinson's poems bring the reader to the brink of the uncreated envisioned as a condition-less condition that eludes all figuration—the mind at the end of its natural existence, at the edge of transitioning "out of nature" once and for all. Like Dickinson in "Because I could not stop for death," Stevens relies on the figurative, though in "Of Mere Being" the figurative declines back tenuously into this world rather than pitching us forward into the next:

> The palm at the end of the mind,
> Beyond the last thought, rises
> In the bronze décor.
>
> A gold-feathered bird
> Sings in the palm, without human meaning,
> Without human feeling, a foreign song.
>
> You know then that it is not the reason
> That makes us happy or unhappy.
> The bird sings. Its feathers shine.
>
> The palm stands on the edge of space.
> The wind moves slowly in the branches.
> The bird's fire-fangled feathers dangle down.[85]

In "Of Mere Being" eternity is at best conceived of as a monochrome adornment at the edge of space—a vision somewhat more reticent than Yeats's gold enameling, mosaics, and drowsy emperors. Instead of Byzantium we have the minimalist version of the opulent Florida characteristic of Stevens's very florid imagination. It is impossible, however, not to see Yeats's golden bird as a direct forebear of Stevens's flagrant peacock. Unlike Yeats's golden bird, Stevens's profligate avian appears to have no capacity (nor any inclination) to sing of what is past or passing or to come. It sings, rather, a song "without human meaning, / without human feeling," a song totally foreign. This is the song of unadulterated decreation, of the uncreated beyond mere being and not reducible to representation. Through the poem's ranging lens, we see its fire-fangled feathers dangling down, a gesture that recalls the ambiguous undulations of Stevens's pigeons at the end of "Sunday Morning" sinking "downward to darkness on extended wings." Yet unlike those pigeons, the palm at the end of the mind rises, which gives a different inflection to the idea of order behind this late Stevens poem. As paradoxically sparse and richly figurative as it is, "Of Mere Being" offers a vision of continuity across the most impossibly discontinuous boundary—the unpassable gulf between our knowing and what exceeds our finite consciousness. Yet, here, too, the palm at the end of the mind and the peacock's fire fangled feathers stand as metaxu, bridges stretching out between the created and the uncreated.

"Distance is the soul of the beautiful," Simone Weil believed, and it is equally the theological principle that allows us to unite with God, though paradoxically for Weil God is unapproachable.[86] Something of that paradox pertains to each of the aforementioned poems, though not one of them is remotely orthodox or even explicitly religious in any way. Dickinson's poems, like Yeats's and Stevens's, exhibit the kind of aesthetic distance conversant of Weil's belief that "a work of art has an author and yet, when it is perfect, it has something which is essentially anonymous about it. It imitates the anonymity of divine art."[87] Up until the limit of this conclusion, each of these poets would concur with Weil's understanding. Art aims at an impersonality, an anonymity, achieved through the life of the poet—the intended, as Yeats would have it, achieved out of accidence. Yet, were one to take that further theological step, one might concur with Weil that just as human art at its best imitates divine art, so "in the same way the beauty of the world proves there to be a God who is both personal and impersonal at the same time, and is neither one nor the other separately."[88] Weil's faith in the continuity between the divine and the world—that which inclines out of nature and that which resides in nature—may well be a step beyond what any poet is prepared to achieve in actuality. Witness the end of Dante's *Paradiso*, where he admits that even his encompassing vision comes up short. Poets cannot stop the generations from dying. Still, it is the paradox of crossing the impassable boundary—nature to mind, mind to mind, and to whatever might lie beyond—that is essential to great poetry even in our own late, fractious, and skeptical time.

This boundary-crossing combination of the personal and the impersonal, the distant and the intimate, typifies great achievement in the art of poetry. In contemporary American poetry, Yusef Komunyakaa's "Facing It" embodies this decreative boundary crossing between self and other, the monumental and the historical, the created and the uncreated, with exemplary awareness of tradition and rueful self-reflection:

> My black face fades,
> hiding inside the black granite.
> I said I wouldn't,
> dammit: No tears.
> I'm stone. I'm flesh.
> My clouded reflection eyes me
> like a bird of prey, the profile of night
> slanted against morning. I turn
> this way—the stone lets me go.
> I turn that way—I'm inside
> the Vietnam Veterans Memorial
> again, depending on the light
> to make a difference . . . .[89]

Komunyakaa's poem begins with a dramatic immediacy that intensifies the personal impact of the drama with the speaker's confession "I said I wouldn't, / dammit. No tears." In addition to setting the scene, the first two lines veritably enact the poet's passage across the decreative boundary from the natural condition of a personal life into the impersonal though nonetheless reflective material of art itself—the Vietnam Veterans Memorial in Washington, DC. The blackness of the speaker's face, both in the remembered literal physical reality of personal history and in the figural present of the poem, enters the very material of Maya Lin's brilliant commemoration of the dead American soldiers of the Vietnam War. Komunyakaa's representation of self, crossing the boundary from life literally into art through the mirroring effect of the monument's material existence, establishes the speaker as simultaneously flesh and stone. Moreover, he appears to exist at once outside and inside the monument and, crucially, it is the poem that continually reenacts and elaborates this double life of the world as it is and the mimetic reflection of the work. Komunyakaa's poem is as much an exploration of art as a process of making and its effect on the observer and the maker as it is a depiction of the work of art.

As the poem progresses it incorporates more details, particular details that would be evanescent if not for their accrual into the life of remembrance that the poem makes present as a monument to the monument it depicts. The slant of night against the morning, the enumeration of the names of the dead evolving in the poem to its focus on the name of one dead soldier known to the speaker who was present at his death, the woman who brushes her blouse, the presence of the white veteran whose glance intermixes with the gaze of the black speaker—all become integrated in every sense into the poem as into the monument. Facing it, the self is threatened with effacement, though the poem's greatest surprise is to transform the threat of effacement into a redressing fulfillment of art's ultimate promise, its hard-won accomplishment:

> A white vet's image floats
> closer to me, then his pale eyes
> look through mine. I'm a window.
> He's lost his right arm
> inside the stone. In the black mirror
> a woman's trying to erase names:
> No, she's brushing a boy's hair.

It is hard not to hear an echo of "There is a certain slant of light" in Komunyakaa's "night / slanted," in view of the difference the light makes shortly afterwards. As in Yeats's "Sailing to Byzantium" and Stevens's "Of Mere Being," a bird appears—more a harbinger than an emblematic figure. Two birds appear in the poem, the first a bird of prey emerging from the speaker's own reflection, evocative of the emotional condition of the survivor before the names of all the dead, an afterimage of bombing missions? Then there is the red bird that cuts across the poet's stare, just a plane in the sky now and not a bird of prey from the past. Komunyakaa's visuals are deftly orchestrated. The monument is at once a mirror and a lamp into the speaker's unconscious life. Seeing is everything in "Facing It," and what we see is how the poem as mirror to another mirroring work of art embodies the reflective power and the light-giving portal of the uncreated within the created world.

The work of art, the poem, as a figure of the uncreated, the mirror of its perfection raised out of accidental natural conditions, at once distorts and clarifies. Or, rather, it calls us to transcend our own proclivity to distort—it provides vantage. The arc of Komunyakaa's poem traces and captures this revisionary vision. His face fades, then reappears, his reflection clouded. If he turns one way the stone lets him go; then he's brought back inside the memorial, he expects to find his own name "like smoke;" the memorial triggers his memory of a death; a woman brushes her blouse, but in the trick of light the names stay on the wall; the white veteran's arm is lost in the stone; and, finally, he thinks a woman is trying to erase the names until he realizes she is only brushing a boy's hair. That final exhilarating perception places us, again, on a threshold—not on the threshold of what is true and what is not true, nor on the threshold of what is outside nature and what is inside it, nor even on the threshold of how everything depends on the relativity of perception. Beyond these, "Facing It" places us on the threshold between life and death, the boundary that if captured by a great work of art has the power to transfigure everything. To embody this boundary, to become a bridge across it, is what poems should seek to accomplish, and thereby enable us to see what is potentially transcendent in our lives through the all too flawed conditions of our lives—to see what transcends as through the glass darkly. This accomplishment, the figure of decreation accomplished paradoxically through the process of creation, is what potentially makes a poem a standard bearer of tradition: the indelible human circumstance embodied as if in stone and handed down. It is how the poem achieves the status of a monument in Yeats's high example, while at the same time remaining a living reality in which we see ourselves reflected, yes, all the dying generations—the poem as granite hard mirror reflecting dark and light, absence and presence, and calling us to see.

5. *Beauty and the Marketplace*

We are standing, my wife and I, on the rooftop of the Metropolitan Museum of Art nursing a pair of specialty martinis. It's happy hour. The bar is crowded. A cross section of well- heeled and middle class humanity, some dressed to the nines, others like my wife and me in jeans looking like true exemplars of our middling economic station, talk in pairs or groups or mill around while the sun begins to set beyond the vast, gradually darkening green of Central Park. The distinctive jagged peaks of Upper West Side apartment buildings appear ramparts in the deeply widening glow, striations of dark and light turning from the lucent white-edged blue to a rich orange-red—a gorgeously ample dimming of the day. A water tower atop one of the taller buildings stands out— wooden, round, and peaked, an artifact of the previous century—amidst the scene which, one imagines, John Singer Sargeant or Edward Hopper might have painted in realist glory, or Mark Rothko might have distilled to an expressively elemental vitality of tones. Now two young women walk over to the western wall, negotiating a clearing in the crowd, each with their back against the scene, each stretching out their arms before them, cell phones in hand, smiling, angling the shot, posing, the scene to which they have their backs a backdrop for their ephemeral portraits, their "selfies." Downstairs, in the galleries, the vital works of cultures and histories—our global, human story told in chosen brilliancies, genius, and remnants—quietly sustain their assumption of the enduring life of art out of the conditions of life into the timeless: the created rendered emblematic of the unconditional—icons of human possibility, a dimension of significance that adds to rather than dismisses the obvious historical and cultural significance of any work.

It is, of course, beautifully genial to be able to look out from the Met roof on a summer twilight, talking with friends, sitting with one's beloved, or milling alone among the crowd. It is a good thing, a fortunate thing. But it also suggests the economic and cultural need for a museum to create allures beyond the works of art themselves, to draw in the "customers" of culture in our latter-day capitalist milieu. The two young women taking selfies engage in the now prevalent act of imprinting self objectively onto potentially every experience. Almost without the mediation of time, much time, that image can be broadcast digitally, globally to friends and total strangers in an eye blink. Compare the self-images of Rembrandt or Van Gogh—"selfies" rendered painstakingly with brush and paint, with the signature of incomparable genius. Where do they stand now in a world where the mass-produced rules and selfies broadcasted digitally offer the illusion of an immediate immortality? Perhaps the juxtaposition is misleading, or disingenuous. I do think the image of those two young women ignoring the sunset for itself alone pitched behind the dramatic cityscape suggests just how much our technologically driven society has altered our relationship to the world, re-centered it around the atomized self, and so altered our relationship to art and to poetry. Paradoxically, in a world in which no story is sustainable, where all stories become the story of no-story, with no metaphysics, no narrative in which self and culture can find the promise of truth, the focus on self, one's sole self and its aggrandizement becomes prevailingly and disturbingly urgent: "I say I want to change the world / but really I want to write poems all day."

We have passed from a world valorized by halls of fame and galleries of great works, among other measures of human aspiration beyond the given materials of life, and have entered what David Bentley Hart in *The Beauty of the Infinite* calls "the marketplace."[90] For Hart, the market as a sign of the times is "not so much a vertical as a horizontal totality, a plane upon which everything can be arranged in a hierarchy of abstract equivalence . . . . It is a totality that contains everything in a state of barren and indifferent plurality."[91] We live in a "spectacle of vanity" in which desire breeds only "the desire to desire more,"[92] in which ideas of achievement measured against tradition and the further discernments of canon appear to self-displace and self-empty—a nullifying kenosis rather than a creative or decreative one. Instead of the free space of expression, the market mind brings into reality "the non-space of non-things, a universal and proliferating immateriality" where judgment, the good discernable from the bad, good from evil, dissipates into consumerism and the prevalence of will: the market powers of the merely fashionable—"this twittering world," as Eliot reflects in "Burnt Norton."

David Bentley Hart's judgment on our current twitter and selfie-driven cultural moment may sound extreme, even reactionary, but it accords well with trends that deemphasize the idea of truth and codify the purely material nature of reality. Pluralism and self-expression become ultimate values, and fame an end in itself. In the realm of contemporary poetry, pluralism—rightly valued—can quickly devolve into the current value-subverting catch phrase, "It's all good." Against this backdrop, heated discussions about aesthetic value appear little more than tempests in teapots—rapidly dissipating tempests in a cracked and leaking, rather antique pot. "To assert the existence of a worldly world," Robert Pinsky observes, "implies there is also a different, distinct world which is other, a spiritual world." Pinsky's apt reflection appears in our own time to be more something of a forced assertion than a trusted confidence. The view of the world's ultimate dependence on a spiritual world[93] is exactly what sustains Hart's painstakingly cogent case for the idea of beauty as being bound to the infinite rather than the fleeting expression of fashion. His critique of postmodernism, and nearly all of post-Enlightenment philosophy, amounts to a refusal of what he calls the "totalizing" rhetoric of meta-narratives, especially the current meta-narrative—the Story of No Truth, the Story of No Stories. Against that meta-narrative, one can posit a defense of tradition that valorizes the story of the beautiful as the story of incarnation through which the infinite is made present and knowable within human life and history. In defense of that vision is the compelling rhetoric of a story that prevails over any philosophical or ideological superstructure. Hart's is a view of tradition sustained as story, a story beside other stories, other traditions, that proposes to redress the fragmentation of the world. In that story, distance, difference, is embraced as part of the enterprise of creation rather than effaced either into a generic unity or an equally bland atomism. Contrarily, he pictures the postmodernist market as the "arid, empty distance that consumes all other distance," a fracturing condition that would reconfigure the vast blazoning of a sunset within the pinpoint frame of self-centeredness.

Admittedly I have forayed from matters of aesthetic discernment into matters better left to theologians, but I do so to place matters of art and tradition within a more fundamental frame of reference and import. Editors and schools of poetry make judgments every day. Reviews are written, anthologies published. Still, what rules if Hart is right is the market, and the market by its nature offers no basis other than its own currency for value, and that currency by its own accounting is counterfeit. Beneath the market's operations will remain "the arid, empty distance" of an atomized cultural condition underlying the aggrandizement of all the many social and private forms of self-advancement. Such workings of the market are nothing new, but what is new is the market's assumption of ultimacy in the absence of any veritable way to bridge the boundaries. In her prophetic way, Simone Weil proposes an alternative conception of artistic distance, the kind of distance whereby the poem exhibits a quality of intention that for all of its uniqueness links it to matters of ultimate value, of truth and—yes—beauty. That is why the greatest art, the greatest poetry, always "imitates the anonymity of divine art."[94] That is why the beautiful always conveys a surplus, a surplus that points beyond itself.

We see this surplus vividly portrayed in Richard Wilbur's great poem, "The Beautiful Changes." Here is the brilliant middle stanza:

> The beautiful changes as a forest is changed
> By a chameleon's tuning its skin to it;
> As a mantis, arranged
> On a green leaf, grows
> Into it, makes the leaf leafier, and proves
> Any greenness is deeper than anyone knows.[95]

The infinite, which Weil would call God, cannot be directly approached, yet we find in Wilbur's remarkable rendering of beauty's ephemeral nature an intimation of life's depths and sustenance in and through the infinite. We approach the infinite through the beautiful, its immediacy and its capacity to mediate an infinite distance—the kind of distance that stretches and expands rather than atomizes and disintegrates. "The Beautiful Changes" captures perfectly that threshold insight, the analogical "spirit level" between kataphasis and apophasis, presence and absence. As Weil recognizes, it is the presence of infinite distance in the creation that establishes the very being of things—the leaf becoming leafier in relation to that which tunes itself to it but which the leaf itself is not—that reveals "the soul of the beautiful."[96]

The powerful idea of beauty as life defining distance finds a rich expression in B.H. Fairchild's poem, aptly titled "Beauty." The poem is a narrative in which the poet, from the considerable distance of age and geography, recalls a time in his youth when he worked in a factory where his father served as foreman. The portrait he paints evokes the same physical, social, cultural, and intellectual curtailments that motivated Weil herself to pursue factory work in order to experience the soul-limiting life of a laborer. In "Beauty" we find the antithetical passage of the worker, having grown unaccountably beyond the given limits, reflecting back on the world of the factory as on a previous existence. What we discover in the poem is beauty as an at first puzzling and finally miraculous expression of distance and healing realized through memory. Here is how the poem opens:

> We are at the Bargello in Florence, and she says,
> *what are you thinking*? And I say, *beauty*, thinking
> of how very far we are now from the machine shop
> and the dry fields of Kansas, the treeless horizons
> of slate skies and the muted passions of roughnecks
> and scrabble farmers drunk and romantic enough
> to weep more or less silently at the darkened end
> of the bar, out of, what else, loneliness, meaning
> the ache of thwarted desire, of, in a word, *beauty*,
> or rather its absence, and it occurs to me again
> that no male member of my family ever used
> this word in my hearing or anyone else's except
> in reference, perhaps, to a new pickup or a dead deer.[97]

This extraordinary opening sentence performs the passage back through time and place of which it speaks, and so underscores the recognition of beauty through the process of one consciousness encountering the mystery of itself, its origins, history, its embrace of a desire for what would enable it to transcend its beginnings. The treeless horizon of Kansas mirrors the internal horizons of the self-reflecting mind—the act of thinking that becomes an act of meaning even in the recognition of limits—the "ache of thwarted desire." Fairchild situates the reader on the vital threshold of a contrast—the beauty of the Bargello

Museum in Florence set in relief of the emptiness and personal loneliness of rural Kansas. Fairchild knows that first world, knows the depth of its limitations and its desperate lives.

As "Beauty" unfolds section by mellifluent section, Fairchild deepens and extends the poem's entry into that retrospective horizon of memory until the poem becomes fully present in its portraiture of the past and the place, the family members and fellow workers, from which the poet has gained such profound distance. Among the most vivid portraits is that of Bobby Sudduth, a foul-mouthed and violent co-worker who runs a Hobbs machine lathe. It is the cutting motion of the lathe that the poem evokes metaphorically, and seeks to redress. "Beauty" would bridge together past and present in a single vision, and with it beauty and ugliness, the transcendence and the emptiness of lives held in the poem's own embracing and restorative fullness. The narrative turns on a single day when two chance new workers enter the shop and inexplicably strip naked before the other men. "I recall how fragile / and pale their bodies seemed against the iron and steel / of the drill presses and milling machines and lathes," Fairchild reflects. In stark contrast to their surroundings, the two naked men take on the startling mantle of art itself:

> . . . in memory they stand frozen
> and posed as two models in a drawing class,
> of whom the finished sketch might be said, though not by me
> nor any man I know, to be beautiful, they stand there
> forever, with the time clock running behind them,
> time running on but not moving, like the white tunnel
> of silence between the snap of the ball and the thunderclap
> of shoulder pads that never seems to come and then
> there it is . . . .

Entering a "forever" figuratively in the middle of time, the men here become figures of artistic figuration—meta-figures embodying the artistic act. By creating this artful meta-space, the poem has made them an incarnation uncreated, lifted out of time and conditions, through time and conditions, by the poet's creative act. What is coming into the poem, from this still point of silence and stop-time, is Bobby Sudduth, an animal terror moving toward them with an iron file—beauty and violence in fraught juxtaposition. It is Fairchild's father who comes between the naked men and their brutal end, touching one of them on his shoulder, saying quietly "you boys will have to go now." Beauty, violence, a tenderness not unlike grace.

In the fourth and final section Fairchild returns to the poem's beginning, now revealing that the speaker is standing with his wife before Donatello's "David," and implying it is this great image of beauty that triggered the memory of the past, his own life story, the naked men in the machine shop on the strangest day anyone who was there will ever remember. He remembers, too, that his father described how Bobby Sudduth shot himself in the chest with a twelve-gauge shotgun, and here, remarkably, at the poem's end, Fairchild paints a vision of past and present sustained in perfect equilibrium, held together in what can only be called a glimpse into the redemptive potential of time itself:

> . . . and so I began
> to tell her about a stranger afternoon in Kansas,
> about something I have never spoken of, and we walk
> to a window where the shining light spreads a sheen
> along the casement, and looking out, we see the city
> blazing like miles of uncut wheat, the farthest buildings
> taken in their turn, and the great dome, the way
> the metal roof of the machine shop, I tell her,
> would break into flame late on an autumn day, with such beauty.

At the end of the poem, distance collapses in a revelation of redemptive seeing that embraces all—the ugliness and violence, the failure of lives, and the mind's gradual passage away from the given conditions, but without loss, and with love: the end in the beginning, the beginning in the end. Though "collapse" is perhaps too strong a verb to describe how Fairchild's poem binds past and present together so vibrantly, to the point of enacting the redemption of the past through the poet's act of imagination. Perhaps a metaphor from astrophysics is better, specifically the phenomenon of gravitational lensing, which is a way of using the gravitational effect of large bodies like galaxies to focus and bring into view even more distant objects whose light is barely visible. "Beauty" rides on a kind of emotional lensing, such that the true gravity of the past emerges into the life of the present and into the reader through the poem: beauty lensing into the entirely beautiful, the distance of the uncreated finding focus in and though the created. Fairchild's portrait of self, past, and place in "Beauty" recalls, again, Weil's insight that the experience of beauty is a manifestation of distance—distance that is the necessary gap that needs to be bridged, that makes possible the bridge that is the poem. From Weil's vantage, as with Fairchild's poem, the beautiful is neither merely pretty nor soothing. The very "ugliness" of a Giacometti sculpture embodies the truth of its beauty, captured in the extremity of a core human monolith of need reaching upward even as the human creature continues perilously forward into the unknown— the vertical bound to the horizontal, that core longing of the species, its cross to bear: the created as incarnation of the uncreated.

This conception of what one might call the poetic ideal finds further practical credence in Louse Glück's "The Wild Iris." There is nothing sentimental about Glück's poetry. Even when flowers speak they do so in a manner that expresses her unsparing vision. "At the end of my suffering / there was a door," so the poem opens, and continues with the voice of one who has returned from the uncreated to speak to the created: "Hear me out: that which you call death / I remember."[98] What we encounter in Glück's poem is something slightly different than Dickinson's post-mortem journey, different again from any figurations, and yet again from beyond a bronze décor hinting at what cannot be represented. The distance Glück's poem traverses it traverses from the uncreated *back* to the created. That is the poem's remarkable fiction. "Terrible," as the voice continues, to survive as "consciousness buried in the dark earth." The vantage, it might be said, is far from Weil's Christian understanding of decreation, but that is not the point. The poem transcends doctrinal limits, just as Weil's heterodox theology (unbaptized as she chose to remain even unto death) cleaves to a transcendence more radical than what falls neatly within more stolidly religious categories. Venturing beyond any such categories, "The Wild Iris" ends with an evocation of beauty, an ultimate ratification of the poem as embodiment of the dynamic interdependence of the created and the uncreated:

> You who do not remember
> passage from the other world
> I tell you I could speak again: whatever
> returns from oblivion returns
> to find a voice:
>
> from the center of my life came
> a great fountain, deep blue
> shadows on azure seawater.

A figure that is found across cultures, throughout history, and in both religious and more secular iterations of the great tradition of poetry and art, the "great fountain" is the embodiment of beauty's inexhaustible source, incarnation as inexhaustible source, recognizable equally to St. John of the Cross and to the Vedas. The voice of "The Wild Iris" communicates poetry's essence understood as a process of decreation. Likewise, tradition, like the individual poem however historically and culturally conditioned, however evolving, acts optimally on some whole or partially enacted form of decreation.

After the year of factory work, after her self-enlistment to fight on the side of Republican forces in the Spanish Civil War, after her spiritual encounter at St. Francis's Chapel in Assisi, after visiting the Benedictine Abbey at Solesmes where she had one of an increasing number of mystical experiences, Weil began reading the English Metaphysical poets and falling in love in particular with George Herbert's "Love III": "Love bade me welcome: yet my soul drew back, / Guilty of lust and sin . . . . " Reading the poem aloud, Weil experienced a profound mystical sensation of Christ's presence, his taking possession of her. It is a testament to the power of great poetry to impact the individual consciousness, and the power of the past to offer itself as "the most perfect image of the eternal, supernatural reality" reaching out to us.[99] Such is the impetus for the poet's labors to contribute to the bridge that is tradition, aiming for something like an image of perfection accomplished in and through the reality of change and necessity and, if not perfection, then an evolving order to which the poet might measure up. Weil's experience of spiritual transformation is a powerful testament to the capacity of Herbert's poem to speak out of the poet's consciousness from another historical moment across the bridge of tradition to someone schooled in a different tongue, a different time, that reveals how the work of art rooted in the conditions of time, place, and personal circumstance can reach beyond its original conditions—through and across those conditions—into the life of another. It is as though it had laid across time and space a bridge from the created to the created through the promise of the uncreated, every separation a link, out of that always partially eclipsed but never wholly obliterated light. Without that light, we have only arbiters of dubitable taste; coercion founded on privilege, or luck, or politics; prevailing myths and the ever-shifting, dimming signs of the times. The varied greatness of our human labors would not have it so, and calls the poet to the halls of something decidedly otherwise and greater.

POETRY AND THE POST-HUMAN, OR
ASHBERY'S FLEAS

1. *No There, There*

Most everything broadcast into the 21st-century home via television or computer, cable, internet, or satellite dish, or outside the home by means of whatever device, iPad or smart phone—eventually an app rigged to one's Raybans or directly into the cerebral cortex—might reasonably be said to fall under the heading of entertainment. Very little of what gets translated from "real life" into digitized scenes through the physically miraculous circuitry that reanimates those scenes before a potentially global audience pressures the receiver toward active contemplation. Or so it seems. In one recent television series, assessable digitally now even on one's smart phone, a compellingly disaffected and quietly brash detective has himself been called into police headquarters to review the narrative circumstances of a series of ritualized serial killings he had investigated seventeen years before. In one riveting scene, the camera fixes on the detective, an avowed nihilist, as he extemporizes before his two stunned interviewers on how the murdered at the moment of their deaths must have welcomed the knowledge that their lives, however lived, good or bad, were nothing more than an illusion; that the very idea of a person was itself an illusion, living as we do on this self-enwound and delusional membrane of existence—all the while carving with his pocket knife, then folding with his fingers a Lone Star beer can into the disposable form of a human being. The scene is entertaining, the writing strong and informed by intellect, the acting compelling, as well as mindfully and emotionally challenging, and disturbing. The scene enacts a vision of reality that has gradually come to dominate intellectual thought and culture, at least in some academic circles, from 19th-century positivism to postmodernism.

The vision assumes, in sum, that all we experience—that consciousness itself—is nothing more than a material phenomenon, a by-product of the physical forces shaping the universe without purpose or goal. Or as the fictional detective muses with as much assurance as a Daniel Dennett or Richard Dawkins, human consciousness is "a chemical mistake." Like the real-life purveyors of populist atheism, he assumes what Marilynne Robinson calls "the one needful thing, the one sufficient account of literally everything."[100] This account, in Robinson's rendering, is little more than a barely veiled monism, a vision of a wholly materialist reality in which accident rules—accident, which Robinson observes inevitably "narrows the range of appropriate strategies of interpretation." "Intention," by contrast, "very much broadens it." One might dare say that intention also deepens our strategizing, our conscious engagement with our human condition, an engagement that refuses to limit us to the shallows of univocal materialism.

Born into these shallows and comfortable within them, our detective is a connoisseur of details and surfaces, an orchestrator of scenarios that enable him to shape the case, if not toward an end—the serial killings have begun again according to the belated investigators—then toward a satisfactory stopping point. He is eminently watchable in his minimalism, a slow walker with his accountant's notebook entering the scene, always finding precisely the sidelong and long smoldering fact. He is a man of few, sometimes outrageous words and, for others, excessively speculative theories—a contrarian, answerable finally to no authority but his own, from police procedure to the law, to God himself in whom he most adamantly does not believe. He is a latter-day version of Nietzsche's Übermensch, scanning clues for intentions that crumble inevitably into accident, which is the groundwork of his anti-metaphysics. And he is an artist of a kind, for whom the appearance of nonpareil abilities bestows the requirement of un-paralleled self-regard, not to mention entitlements due only to the truly exceptional. He is a figure of unique qualities, yet those qualities somehow appear familiar, accustomed as we have become to the artist as the embodiment of incomparable and incorrigible Genius, self-proclaimed.

Among the moderns there are surely artists and poets who conform to the broad profile—titanic ego fueling unstoppable ambition. Then again, for all of his arrogance even Pound had in mind a project that would restore, at least among the chosen few, some semblance of human culture at its most highly achieved. For all his bravado, his aims had motive and real depth—the hope of an achievement beyond his own monumental aspirations, which is undoubtedly why he became such a staunch advocate for other poets and artists. Civilization, botched, depended on an artistic remnant. Perhaps, however, Picasso makes a better match, driven as he was by a libidinous narcissism exceeded only by his genius. Still, to browse through a retrospective of Picasso's immense oeuvre is to recognize that from his childhood he had mastered the history of Western art. Picasso was a master Renaissance painter by the time he was a teenager. His radical departures into Cubism and beyond find their source in those deep roots. Of that early 20th-century circle of greats, Gertrude Stein appears to measure up most perfectly to the idea of the artist as self-announced genius unimpeded by the past, without allegiance to any binding vision of life beyond the will to make art. Here is an artist content to play among the vivid surfaces of language and reality without any other justification save for her consummate self-regard and the presumption of entitled fame. No wonder Stein is widely regarded as the matriarch of so much contemporary American avant-garde poetry. To venture an unlikely paraphrase from Robert Frost's "The Gift Outright," Stein was ours before we were Stein's. Her way of writing and her way of being is in many ways her gift outright to so much contemporary poetry.

Gertrude Stein's self-appointed and self-engineered destiny to ascend the literary world of her time had been nascent from the earliest age. "Our Gertie is a little Schnatterer," her aunt Rachel reflected in a letter to her father who had returned to America from Vienna in search of business success, "she is such a round little pudding, toddles around the whole day & and repeats everything that is said or done."[101] Decades later, Wyndham Lewis took up aunt Rachel's "Schnatterer" theme when he characterized Stein's writing as the work of an "idiot child, but none the less sweet to itself for that," who "throws big, heavy words up and catches them; or letting them slip through its fingers they break in pieces; and down it squats with a grunt, and begins sticking them together again."[102] Lewis's devastating judgment on Stein's "infantile" method of writing would seem starkly at odds with Stein's life history. She was one of William James's devotees at Harvard, a promising medical student at Johns Hopkins who was constitutionally incapable of pursuing a directed course of study, and then an art collector and self-taught writer who would become a literary and cultural force—the "Sybil of Montparnasse," hosting the likes of Picasso, Hemingway, Fitzgerald, and Matisse, among many others—before emerging as a world-famous innovator who declared herself one of the three great geniuses of her time. The others were Picasso and Alfred North Whitehead. Certain she was the greatest prose-writer of her age, she judged herself more accomplished than Joyce, her nearest rival. By her own accounting, she regarded herself perhaps greater even than Shakespeare. "He's dead," she declared, "and can't say whether he's greater than I am. Time will tell."[103]

Despite her penchant for self-promotion, it is now acknowledged that her brother Leo was in fact rather than legend the brilliantly prescient collector of works by Cézanne, Matisse, Picasso, and many others before their genius had been widely recognized. They parted ways, Gertrude and Leo, on the significance of Cubism, which Leo believed had ludicrous origins in Picasso's "childishly silly" misreading of mathematics.[104] Their parting became permanent when Alice B. Toklas assumed Leo's place as confidant and friend. Sister and brother would barely acknowledge each other after 1914, the year of their "disaggregation."[105] With the publication of *The Autobiography of Alice B. Toklas*, Matisse, Tristan Tzara, and others accused Stein of flagrantly "legendizing" her life, levying claims of egomania, megalomania, and outright literary prostitution against her. Leo Stein called the book a "farrago of rather clever anecdote, stupid brag and general bosh."[106] In response, Stein claimed history was not "something you remember" but something one is bound to recreate, and so she felt no "obligation to remember right."[107] At the crux of Gertrude Stein's riposte to her detractors, former friends, and fellow artists is a conception of identity that anticipates a valuation of consciousness acutely tuned to the materialism of more than a few modern and contemporary philosophers of mind. Here is Stein's reflection on the subject:

> And identity is a funny being yourself is funny you are never yourself except as you remember yourself and then of course you do not believe yourself. That is really the trouble with an autobiography you do not really believe yourself why should you, you know so well so very well that it is not yourself, it could not be yourself because you cannot

remember right and if you do remember right it does not
sound right and of course it does not sound right because it
is not right. You are of course never yourself.[108]

Stein's headlong associative stream of propulsive redundancy in this excerpt
from *Everybody's Autobiography* not only typifies her prose style, it exemplifies
a vision of self as something fundamentally discontinuous and illusory—if
not a chemical mistake then a wholesale fabrication, or phantom. Self is an
illusion, and so by extension, self-invention is the primary requirement of the
autobiographer. If one's personal history is gotten wrong, or let us say enhanced,
so be it—identity may be our most amendable fiction. Disagreements as to
the promulgated veracity of the past will, by extension, arise simply out of
the variance of individual memories, all of which are inventions of selves that
are never really themselves to begin with. Legend, as Stein's biographer Janet
Hobhouse reflects, becomes more "potent" than "true history."[109] Regardless of
the validity of this underlying concept of identity, or the actual history of events
and persons in Stein's life, *The Autobiography of Alice B. Toklas* had a profound
impact: "The book bulldozed its way through facts and sensibilities and had
arrived triumphant on the other side of the destruction." In short, it made "its
own truth."[110] In Stein's version of "alternative facts," art trumps life since life,
for Stein, exists exclusively for art.

There is something eerily determined in Stein's life portrait from her
childhood as family "Schnatterer" through her years after the *Autobiography*
when she had become a living literary legend, and onward through her life
in occupied France during the Second World War, and onward still until
her death from stomach cancer in 1946. Along with her determination for
acquiring fame, Stein had a great love for meeting people, and not only (though
especially) famous people—geniuses or would-be geniuses who might come
near to, though not exceed, her own incomparable brilliance. She and Alice
worked as nurses' aids during the First World War, and she liked the soldiers,
and especially liked the song "On the Trail of the Lonesome Pine," which
she heard them sing. While living at Belley under Marshall Petain during
the Second World War, one of her neighbors observed how intently Stein

would analyze people so as to find "the secret that motivated their action."[111] According to her biographer, this imperative accords with her early love of archetypes, those similarities and differences between people as exemplified in *Three Lives* and *The Making of Americans*, the "rhythm of personality" she sought to portray in her portraits of Picasso and others, and in the calculating descriptions of friends and family. "Her loyalties and her passions were always for ideas or for ideas of people, and rarely for people themselves," Hobhouse concludes.[112] Undoubtedly Alice B. Toklas was a singular exception, though during her soirees Stein held court with the great men of her time while Alice was relegated to stay with the wives. In one memorable scene during the Second World War, Alice, the beloved "Mama Woojums" to Stein's "Baby Woojums," was told by the great artist to move a cow continually at different angles around a pasture in the French countryside in order for Stein to write down the various impressions in the manner of a Cubist painter at work. There is no record of how Alice felt about the day's job—one expects she accepted the role—and the cow must have been happy to eat whatever grass regardless of the positioned angle relative to the writer at work. Not far off, great armies were moving across Europe, soldiers dying, Jews displaced and transported to death camps.

Stein's tendency to elide the individual for the idea of the individual, like her tendency to elide the reality of identity for the idea of identity, defines the unstinting opacity of her writing. More than being about a cow in a pasture, about Picasso or Matisse or the various "objects" in the prose poems of *Tender Buttons*, her writing is about writing. One senses the world is really nothing more than an occasion for more writing. Identity, in turn, is nothing more than an abstraction from that which paradoxically does not really exist, at least to any extent that requires genuine regard. Such willfully recondite distancing from life defines her relationship to the traumatic events of World War II and the Holocaust, through which she lived in a condition of protected adjacency. "A war is always not so very near. Even when it is near," she wrote in *Wars I Have Seen*.[113] Exiled safely from her Paris apartment, while living in Belley and then Culoz, she became a staunch royalist and supporter of Marshall Petain, leader of Nazi occupied France. In 1944, she was translating his speeches and hoped to obtain an American readership for them—this, just as the Jewish children of Culoz were being loaded off to Auschwitz.[114] The war was near, but not so very near, apparently. Years before, in 1934, in a piece published in the *New York Times*, Stein called for Hitler to receive the Nobel Peace Prize "because he is removing all elements of contest and struggle from Germany. By driving out the Jews and the democratic left elements, he is driving out everything that conduces to activity. That means peace."[115] While Stein's endorsement of Hitler for the Noble Peace Prize is often interpreted as an instance of her acute penchant for irony, given the vicious realities and Stein's own Jewish heritage, one would think that this ironic clarion would be regarded, at best, as tasteless.

It is disturbing. It is, in fact, the measure of an artist whose colossal ego and entitlements establish her on the sanitized side of protective glass, coddled by privilege, self-regard, and abstracted from life by an art that had been purified of life, and by an idea of art that cares little if anything for the actual human being. In "Four Saints," Saint Theresa answers Stein's question "If it were possible to kill five thousand chinamen by pressing a button would it be done?" by responding: "Saint Theresa is not interested." Were one to read *The Interior Castle*, one would know the real Saint Theresa, drawn to the living flame of contemplation though earth-bound, would answer with horror and consternation, nevermind the words put in her mouth by her modern "Sibyl." She would, on the contrary, answer out of the spirit of love which is always committed to life, life emergent (in her view) from the Source of life. Stein's Saint Theresa, responding as she does in the third person—the same way Stein speaks of herself in *The Autobiography of Alice B. Toklas*—is nothing more than a faux mouthpiece for the writer. That is, for her art and the importance it bestows upon her. The death of masses is uninteresting. Here, in turn, is how Stein in her statement on the matter regards people: "Anybody can know that the earth is covered all over with people. . .there are an awful lot of them anyway and in a way I am really interested only in what genius can say the rest is just there anyway."[116] All the earth and its persons are expendable for the purpose of genius, relegated for use by the designs of genius—her genius, genius that paradoxically exists absent of any viable belief in personal identity.

Stein's genius, or the mode of her pioneering and radically obsessive writing habits, blossomed with her recognition that literary composition could be made to enact the kind of disaggregating approaches to form exemplified in the work of Cézanne, Picasso, and Juan Gris. Fundamentally, the shift involved privileging the dimension of space over the dimension of time, effectively the transposition of a painter's spatial orientation to the work of composition into the temporal medium of the literary work. First practiced in *Three Lives* and to some degree or another in every work thereafter, with the exception of *The Autobiography of Alice B. Toklas*, Stein's approach required the suppression of the flow of past, present, and future into the shaping of a "prolonged present." As she notes in "Composition as Explanation":

> A composition of a prolonged present is a natural composition in the world as it has been these thirty years it was more and more a prolonged present. I created then a prolonged present naturally I knew nothing of a continuous present but it came naturally to me to make one, it was simply it was clear to me and nobody knew why it was not done like that, I did not myself although naturally to me it was natural.[117]

Sadly, there is in fact very little real explanation in Stein's recounting of her theory of composition. The passage performs in a somewhat more restricted manner the slow-motion effect of her "continuous present" even as the run-on sentence careens headlong ahead while it doubles back on itself and its subject in an obsessively propulsive redundancy. Here is a more emphatic example from the same lecture:

> Everything is the same except composition and as the composition is different and always going to be different everything is not the same. Everything is not the same as the time when of the composition and the time in the composition is different. The composition is different, that is certain.[118]

Yes, the composition would appear to be quite different, though perhaps not entirely intelligible, or perhaps something like a continuous turning over of the surface of things, the plowing over of things in the shallows, only to find only more, only more, and more and more surface, more shallows, though the aim apparently was to get at "the bottom nature of things" through a strategy of pervasive repetition. Here is the famous opening of her portrait of Picasso:

> One whom some were certainly following was one who was completely charming. One whom some were certainly following was one who was charming. One whom one was following was one who was completely charming. One whom some were following was one who was certainly completely charming.[119]

The point to be made by citing these few examples—Stein wrote a nine-hundred-page composition of her continuous present in *The Making of Americans*—is that each composition is not really different from any other. Stein's approach and its net effect is always the same, the gist of which is exactly contrary to the effect of the great painters from which Stein drew inspiration. Where Cézanne and the Cubists "strove to make non-narrative form convey a sense of movement in time, the continuous present was an attempt to suspend the passage of time in narrative form."[120] In essence, Stein's defining compositional effect enacts a view of reality that elides time as an expression of meaningful depth:

> It is very interesting that nothing inside them, that is when you consider the very long history of how every one ever acted or has felt, it is very interesting that nothing inside in them, that is when you consider in all of them makes it connectedly different. By this I mean this. The only thing that is different from one time to another is what is seen and what is seen depends on how everybody is doing everything.[121]

That which is seen, the surface, is all, all that really is, and only is. There is no inside distinguishing anyone who ever lived from anyone else who ever lived ever, one might again say in the Stein fashion. It would seem then that "the bottom nature" Stein would plumb so deftly and deeply is bottomless not because it is infinite in depth but in fact because it is all only surface.

Stein's ambition to suspend time in narrative form, to create a continuous present, trespasses on still more significant philosophical and theological issues. Some sixteen hundred years before Stein desired to create a continuous present, Augustine of Hippo in his *Confessions* reflected on the impossibility of accessing anything like the present, given the inevitable flow of time. "Who can lay hold on the heart and give it fixity," Augustine muses, "so that for some little moment it may be stable, and for a fraction of time may grasp the splendor of a constant eternity?"[122] The answer, as Christine Casson rightly states, is either no one or God, since, for Augustine, "there is no way that God's eternity and the human experience of 'temporal successiveness' . . . can be compared."[123] Nonetheless it is the mind's ability to expect, attend, and remember—to engage in the work of intending meaning in a manner so as to hold together past, present, and future—that allows an individual to conceive of discrete actions or events as parts of a whole, the narrative of a life that is nonetheless distended, held, in God's eternity.[124] Stein's continuous present inverts Augustine's model of narrative form. By effacing the temporal movement fundamental to narrative and human experience, her continuous present constructs a distorted if not false mirror image of Augustine's "constant eternity." The result is an experience where time continually folds back on itself as one moves forward in "the experiential space" of reading. A Cubist painting by Braque or Picasso need not worry about narrative time in the same manner, obviously, only multiple vectors or angles or planes within space, while Duchamp's "Nude Descending Staircase," for example, at once parses and stretches narrative action into the space of the canvas. Narrative, and even the lyric, which arguably seeks to launch into the timeless, ultimately establishes "a reversal of expectations," for it is "in time that imagination configures meaning."[125] To presume to establish a continuous present, a constant eternity in a medium established definitively by temporal means—language—is delusional at face value, a misapplication of design strategies from the plastic arts. From a theological standpoint, it might be considered a form of idolatry. However one regards the creation of a continuous present, it is certainly not "a new composition in the world," as Stein claimed.

St. Augustine notwithstanding, and despite Stein's Cubist prose, Picasso did not hold with Stein's view that she and he were the two great artistic geniuses of their time. When Stein's brother Leo communicated her view and her intent to use words like paint or verbal collage, the master Picasso shrugged his shoulders and said, "That sounds rather silly to me. With lines and colors one can make patterns, but if one doesn't use words according to their meaning they aren't words at all."[126] Alfred Kazin, Edmund Wilson, Katherine Anne Porter, and Wyndham Lewis all reflect on the child-like monotone of Stein's work, as well as the absence of real emotion, though Kazin's insight that Stein really has very little concern for the subject of the work or the objective nature of the real strikes deepest. "The book" is merely "a receptacle for her mind," he rightly concludes.[127] For Kazin, Stein's early life "schnattering" only got more sophisticated, more marketable. By contrast, Alfred Stieglitz genuinely embraced and extolled her experiments. In any case, regardless of her detractors and her rather shameless efforts at self-aggrandizement, or perhaps because of them, Stein has become a literary touchstone, a principal bridge linking modernism to postmodernism. She is the mater familias of the contemporary zeitgeist extolling dissociative and elliptical poetry, the zeitgeist that proclaims to have won the day, at least as exemplified in a great many academic programs and prominent journals. One example from *Tender Buttons* will show why. Here is "Apple":

> Apple plum, carpet steak, seed clam, colored wine, calm seen, cold cream, best shake, potato, potato and no gold work with pet, a green seen is called bake and change sweet is bready, a little piece is a little piece please.
> A little piece please. Cane again to the presupposed and ready eucalyptus tree, count out sherry and pie plates and little corners of a kind of ham. This is use.[128]

The apple as an object in the world has no place in Stein's prose poem. It exists only as a word that triggers a sequence of disassociated associations linked mostly sonically, sound used in the way a painter employs paint—all fricatives, plosives, and labials bounding off each other with long and short vowels. The final declarative, "This is use," must be read ironically, for there is no use for this apple except for the usage just given: this unique mélange of language on the page savored, perhaps, by the mental tongue. It is a marvelously child-like performance, depthless, happily free of worldly identification, just as identity is free of any pretense of subjectivity or history. The poem exists in the continuous present of the writer's arrangement of non-sequiturs, which is the product of the one mind, evidently, that counts: her own. One can see why a prospective publisher in Stein's early writing years might shy away from accepting such a composition for publication, as was the case with one A.C. Fifield of London in 1912, the year *Tender Buttons* was published. His rejection is a brilliant parody of the Stein mode:

> Dear Madam,
>
> I am only one, only one, only one. Only one being, one at the same time, not two, not three, only one. Only one life to live, only sixty minutes in one hour. Only one pair of eyes. Only one brain. Being only one, having only one pair of eyes, having only one time, having only one life, I cannot read your M.S. three or four times. Not even one time. Only one look, only one look is enough. Hardly one copy would sell here. Hardly one. Hardly one.
>
> Many thanks. I am returning the M.S. by registered post. Only one M.S. by one post.[129]

Fifield's witty rejection mimes marvelously Stein's practiced monotony, and puts one in mind of the inestimable Professor Irwin Corey, comic master of brilliant-sounding gibberish on many television shows during the 1960s, and who billed himself as "The World's Foremost Authority." Fifield's wry response rightly fixates on time, the very dimension that Stein was so interested in submerging in her writing. Despite the temptation to elaborate the parodies, one must concede that Stein surely has had the last laugh. Indeed, she has marketed her "legendary genius" and her work to a great many poets more than a generation after her death, regardless of initial critical dismay and her own disaggregation from family and prominent friends. The scions of Stein's artistry and example now far outnumber, or out theorize—those who vilify her, and her champions fill the ivory towers. Tony Hoagland, an American poet very unlike Gertrude Stein, praises her in a recent essay as an "American Master," where he rightly describes her work's appeal as "largely decorative." By the idea of composition, Hoagland reflects, Stein "means giving up the semantic imperative of language . . . . She means using words like musical notes, or paint, a plastic material in relative weight determined by sound and placement, not by meaning."[130] Her work advances an "indefinite" suggestiveness.

Precisely on target, Hoagland's characterization neglects to point out the self-evident fact that poets who follow "the semantic imperative," if they are good practitioners of the art and certainly if they are masters, also use words with all the care of composers and painters. In extolling Stein, Hoagland in effect affirms the sad condition of how little we have come to expect of our masters. "I like the idea of Gertrude Stein," one editor of a prominent literary journal remarked to me once, "but I cannot read her." There is no there, there, Gertrude Stein famously said of Oakland upon her return to her childhood home during her triumphant visit to America after she had become a household name. One might say the same about her work—no inward identity, only self-proclaimed genius, no outward reality, only words toggled to the language system, no there except for what is there—there, there—the world, indefinite, flat, bereft, composed of surfaces turning over again and again in the shallows to nothing more than more surface, faceless, masterfully lessened out of all amplitude.

2. *In the Manner Of*

There is a photograph of Gertrude Stein taken in occupied France during the Second World War. She is standing in the doorway of what looks to be an ancient chapel dressed in a flowing white robe, as though she were a monk or priestess and where she stood was the portal to the altar where she performs her secret rites. To her left is a friend, Bernard Fay, who was among the small, late coterie of admirers; to her right, Alice B. Toklas. Both are sitting on a stone wall, both looking rather pressed into service in what is obviously a posed scene. Behind them and behind the self-proclaimed genius as High Priestess is the magnificent French countryside where, not very far beyond the orchestrated setting, Jews are being herded for transport to the concentration camps and gas chambers of the east, just as they had been in Paris not far from Gertrude and Leo Stein's celebrated apartment at 27 rue de Fleurus, her art collection protected and intact while the Nazis were stealing thousands upon thousands of the greatest art works in the history of the West and hoarding them in mines under threat of destruction should they lose the war. The camera's stage set looks like a moment excised from history, a continuous present in which the pointed cap of the chapel rising from the roof's steep, sloping braid appears like some outsized miter, the headdress that frames the holy figure at the center. The scene is obsessively framed, even mannered. At the doorjamb behind, a few boards lean haphazardly, and from further behind in the dark hutch of stone, light strains to enter through a broken window. The path coming on the scene is weed-strewn. The chapel is a ruin.

It is no great insight to point out that artists, even great artists, are often deeply flawed and occasionally egregiously flawed human beings, egocentric, megalomaniacal, willing sometimes to trade human sensitivity for self-aggrandizement. Some would say such behavior is excusable, even a necessity for the art to have been produced at all. Beyond this commonplace, what interests me is how the poet's vision of life infuses and shapes the work, however much the life may or may not be influenced by the vision of life explicitly or implicitly espoused. During her American tour in 1927, as she rode the glory of *The Autobiography of Alice B. Toklas,* Stein repeated from her lecture "Composition as Explanation" that "the business of art is to live in the complete actual present" and, moreover, that "words have come to lose their meanings" over the last hundred years. What excited her was "that the words or words that make what I look at be itself were always words that to me," she said, "were very exactly related themselves to the thing the thing at which I was looking, but as often as not had as I say nothing whatever to do with what any words would do to describe the thing."[131] For Stein's biographer it is precisely this misalliance between word and thing that belied a "mystic closeness" beneath the obscurity so endemic, in particular, to her poetry.[132] "Poetry," for Stein, "has to do with vocabulary," just as prose, for her, does not.

Poetry is "really loving the name of anything and that is not prose," she declares in "Poetry and Grammar." And she continues: "so as I say poetry is essentially the discovery, the love, the passion for the name of anything."[133] How does one align the inherent misalliance between thing and word to the poet's essential love for the name of a thing? The answer is, one cannot. Or as Stein goes on to say of *Tender Buttons,* "Was there not a way of naming things that would not invent names, but means names without naming them."[134] In short, "the thing had to be named without using its name," since the name of anything "is no longer anything to thrill anyone except children."[135] Simply put, for Stein, a poet's naming always trumps the names of things since the names of things have become outmoded. "A rose is a rose is a rose is a rose," Stein famously wrote, and she regarded it as the first time in over a hundred years that the rose appeared vitally in a line of poetry. William Butler Yeats might have disagreed, since words for him possessed something akin to magical powers, amplitudes of meaningful affiliation, as in his "Rose Upon the Rood of Time."

Of course, for Stein, the point is that a rose is not a rose, the thing is not its name. With this assertion, she puts into artistic practice the difference between thing and word advanced by linguist Ferdinand de Saussure. Stein's view of language also anticipates Derrida's philosophical position later in the 20th century. Both hold that difference rather than identity shapes the operations of language as a system of signs. By now, to a substantial extent, the misalliance assumed by Stein a hundred years ago has been institutionalized as one of the guiding tenets of postmodernism. At root is a disruption in relation between word and thing, sign and signified, and as such between one thing and another. In Picasso's words, words cease to be words at all if we understand the nature of words requires the meaningful relation to things. For Stein, the given names of things are dead on arrival. Those fragments shored against ruins of which Eliot spoke in *The Waste Land,* and which he sought to bind back together in the religious quest of his later poems, are the very evanescent stuff from which Stein happily shapes her poems. The same is the case, implicitly if not explicitly, for many poets from Stein through Ashbery and onward to a crowded house of postmodernist poets. Likewise, the vision of life undergirding art is the very antithesis of William Carlos Williams's "no ideas but in things," since ideas are composed of words, and words and things exist only within the fabricated relationship established through the conventions of language's system of signs—words touch nothing, relate to nothing.

One might demure from the more epistemological and ontological implications of Stein's practice and choose to say that she was like Pound, in his way only trying to "make it new." Nevertheless, as with Saussure and Derrida, at the foundation of Stein's vision is the most extreme outgrowth of nominalism, the complete embrace of the essential breakage between the names we use and the reality we perceive. And no path back to the realist's ideal that words can communicate universals. While some forty years ago Robert Pinsky proclaimed the ultimate goal of the nominalist poem is "logically impossible" because it assumes that "the gap between language and experience is absolute,"[136] and therefore the poet's experience becomes "ungeneralizable" into poems, it is nonetheless the case that over the same period such poems have become commonplace in journals, on websites, and promulgated by small and large presses alike. The nominalist poet has become "impossibly" but pervasively institutionalized in the academy under the nomenclature and orthodoxy of postmodernism.

In his most recent edition of *Postmodern American Poetry*, the latest of two tradition-establishing anthologies, Paul Hoover affirms the preeminence of "postmodern" poetry when he writes, "as it happens with every generation the new wins the day and the broader writing culture is altered by its theories and its practices."[137] With the hiring of avant-garde poets to teach in MFA programs and English departments, with the space afforded to postmodernist poetry in journals and presses, websites, and its prominent distribution through the Academy of American Poets, it is obvious Hoover is right: the postmodernist poem has "come to be considered a reigning style."[138] The so-called "elliptical poets," celebrated by Stephanie Burt in her *Close Calls with Nonsense*, as well as younger poets who embrace "the skittery poem of our moment," to use Tony Hoagland's apt phrase, all fall under the broad category of "postmodern" as Hoover uses the term. I prefer to call such poems *postmodernist*, reserving the more neutral term *postmodern* historically for poems written after the modernist movement, possibly integrating some of its strategies and effects, and combining them with a variety of traditional and non-traditional approaches. Hoover, on the other hand, regards the term *postmodern* as synonymous with the avant-garde of the early 20th century. But if the postmodern is so widely established, how can it still be considered avant-garde? Postmodernist poetry as the established go-to mode traces its early practice to Gertrude Stein's "egalitarian theory of composition," and her own example from Cézanne in which one thing is as important as another thing in the process of composition.[139] Paradoxically, that very egalitarian mode involves an experimental approach that "sets itself apart from mainstream culture and the narcissism, sentimentality and self-expressiveness of its life in writing."[140] Apparently, for Hoover, egalitarian theories of composition can also be elitist relative to mainstream culture without contradiction.

As I noted earlier, Stein was anything but egalitarian, and her approach to her art betrays her elitism. The one exception is *The Autobiography of Alice B. Toklas*, which enabled her to reap the spoils of a longed-for fame. Nonetheless, if Stein has become the mater familias of what has become the apparent mainstream of contemporary American poetry, then the pater familias would have to be Charles Olson, whom Hoover tells us coined the word "postmodern" in a letter to Robert Creeley in 1951.[141] Like Stein, Olson sought to free writing from what he perceived to be a worn-out traditionalism. Like Stein, space for Olson takes precedence over time through the positing of the page as "an open field" that, paradoxically, liberates the poet from "print bred" composition, or so he argues in "Projective Verse."[142] Distribution of words on a page's space, according to Olson, is better suited to registering the poem's voice than traditional forms, the "ancient salt", as Yeats called it. Hoover recognizes rightly that these progenitors along with their postmodernist offspring all hold certain stated or unstated assumptions in common, despite variations in practice and accomplishment, from so- called "aleatory poetics" to L=A=N=G=U=A=G=E poetry to Flarf. All, at root, are nominalist in their understanding of reality and language (though not all postmodern poets need embrace the nominalist vision, and many do not). Here is Hoover on the fundamental tenets of postmodernism:

Postmodernism decenters authority and embraces pluralism.

> It encourages a panoptic or many-sided point of view.
> Postmodernism prefers "empty words" to the "transcendental
> signified," the actual to the metaphysical . . . . With the death
> of God and the author, appropriation becomes a reigning
> device . . . . Thus the material of art is to be judged simply as
> material, not for its transcendent meaning or symbolism.[143]

The epistemological disjuncture that inevitably ensues when nominalism becomes reified into its own ideology—our natural and welcome doubt about our ability to obtain some truth transformed into a hard-line way of seeing and being—finds its ontological mirror image in a thoroughgoing materialism. The philosophical forefathers of this vision of reality include, according to Hoover, Nietzsche, Heidegger, Foucault, and Derrida. The collective intellectual fuel that drives the engine behind the poetry affirms that "Eternity was driven out completely," that "Eternity is reduced to Ethernity, the cybernetic universe that can be shared by all, much of which is mundane and profane. It is not that postmodernism lacks foundations, as some have suggested, but rather that the foundations have shifted from the transcendent to the everyday."[144] Another way to state this is in the words of Tam Lin: "Poetry = wallpaper." Oh, if only we didn't have to read poetry at all, but if it could just be looked at, like a placemat.[145]

There are a number of glaring contradictions embedded in Hoover's panegyric to the loss of Eternity and postmodernism's artistic and ethical triumph over the gutted corpse of outmoded metaphysics. Most glaring is the contradiction that claims a foundation for postmodernism in "the everyday" when "the everyday" lacks any underlying coherence. If language does not connect us to the world or to itself, then how can one posit a foundation to the everyday, whatever that might be? That would have to be a foundation-less foundation, which again, sadly needful to say, is a self-contradiction. Another contradiction is the foregrounding of process and procedure over "product," when it is precisely books (or something analogous to books)—in short, *products*—that are produced, blurbed, marketed, celebrated, and which obtain for the, apparently, identity-less author an agreeable salary at an institution of higher learning where he or she can teach other would-be identity-less authors to produce additionally elaborated processes we conventionally agree to call poems. Elsewhere Hoover invokes Frederic Jameson and his belief that history "ends" with liberal democracy. He also invokes our culture of consumerism as a cause of "the blank style," as the inspiration for many conceptual poets, and as the instigator of "language poetry's preference for Stein's continuous present."[146] If all this is true, how is it that postmodernist poetry can set itself apart from the mainstream when, by Hoover's own analysis, postmodernism is now an expression of the mainstream? Such poetry could be nothing more than a reiteration of the times, an empty mimesis composed in self-emptying words to express a cultural emptiness, all the product of passing consciousness, itself "a chemical mistake."

To heap contradiction upon contradiction, if as Hoover states the avant-garde "opposes the bourgeois model of consciousness," which is apparently inherently narcissistic, sentimental, and concerned wholly with self-expression, unlike postmodernism, how is it John Ashbery, the paragon of postmodernist poetry—the essential poet of "indeterminacy" whose work embodies in its "disembodied" way all the prime features of its kind—how is it that Ashbery's work can be said approvingly to point "toward a new mimesis, with consciousness as its model"?[147] Like Stein, Ashbery does not paint a picture of the apple; he paints a picture of the mind "at work rather than the objects of attention."[148] Is Ashbery's consciousness something other than bourgeois, a different model entirely? If so, how is this model of consciousness to be conceived of without language cohering sufficiently to posit something like a world, however skeptically we might regard that world? Perhaps Charles Bernstein provides the answer in his essay "Thought's Measure," a theoretical classic of Language poetry:

> Language is the material of both thinking and writing. We think and we write in language, which sets up an intrinsic connection between the two.
> Just as language is not something that is separable from the world, but rather is the means by which the world is constituted . . . . It is through language we experience the

world, indeed through language that meaning comes into
the world and into being . . . . I do not suggest that there
is nothing beyond, or outside of, human language, but
that there is meaning only in terms of language, that the
givenness of language is the givenness of the world.[149]

Bernstein's reflection on language, thinking, and the world advances the
nominalist vision of reality with utmost precision. The world is constructed
in language, which also constructs our thinking. What the world may be in
itself—that beyond—is not accessible through language. It is the one a priori,
utterly bound to its conventions, without relation to anything objective,
since the world as given is subjectively formed in thinking, in consciousness,
which is necessarily bound to the materiality of language. One might say
with Bernstein that the model of consciousness in an Ashbery poem, or any
nominalist poem, is nothing other than thinking seeking to narrow its prospect
as much as possible to the materiality of language itself which, because of its
utter conventionality (its separateness from whatever world might be beyond),
is necessarily contingent, arbitrary, depthless. It is poetry as "word-system," as
Marjorie Perloff calls it in *The Poetics of Indeterminacy*, where she describes
Stein's poem "Susie Asado" as a superposition of verbal planes that create "a
kind of geometric fantasy" of the kind one finds in Picasso's Cubist paintings.[150]
Language is not a lamp, nor is it a mirror. It is more like a quantum fabric
raised to the macro-level of reality, skittery in its uncertainty. Poems exemplify
nothing more than the "free play" of the language system, "constructing"
as Perloff observes "a way of happening rather than an account of what has
happened, a way of looking rather than a description of how things look."[151]

At the same time, in an observation that anticipates Hoover's self-
contradictory claims about postmodernism, Perloff informs us that Stein's use
of repetition and variation creates meaning's indeterminacy by establishing
"semantic gaps" in the text, and thus her syntax "enacts the gradually changing
present of human consciousness, the instability of emotion and thought."[152] Yet
how can the word-system of a poem enact a mimesis of consciousness when
the system is self-enclosed? So fundamental a confusion appears endemic to

postmodernist discourse, for in pressing her point further she affirms Stein's *Tender Buttons* summarily performs the slippage of "signifier to signifier" even as the poet's mind plays before the world, such that words, "pliable, come alive in the quick of consciousness." Somehow the word as signifier makes a quantum leap outside the system and comes to exist in concert with the "play" of the poet's mind in "the quick of consciousness?"[153] At the same time, reality, the world, is a mere matter of individual construction, to underscore Bernstein's point. One might hesitate to call this a world at all, but a self-enclosed matrix of belated meaning, meaning endlessly deferred, divorced from the relational and essentially gestural origins in the life of the body.[154] In this unmade world, the word has unmade the flesh, thereby unmaking itself.

From this vantage, the new model of consciousness behind the established conventions of postmodernist poetry reveals mind to be a selfless Narcissus whose every meaning evaporates in a fog of slippages. Rather than poetry founded on genuine plurality, relational in the substance of reality however flowing, inherently gestural, we have poetry impoverished, devolving to endless variations on the same univocal assumption, so many poems at once emerging from and skittering to the same final destination: an I that doesn't exist in a world that cannot be represented. In such an aesthetic, poems become the expressionless expressions of those slippages regardless of authorial intent, even if there were any such thing as an author at all.

"The relation between the sign and the thing signified is being destroyed," Simone Weil reflected early in the 20th century with characteristic prescience, a circumstance that she believed leads inevitably to a variety of non-thought masquerading as thinking—a kind of faux thinking.[155] Any true believer in the epistemological and ontological agenda of the postmodernist would say that is precisely the point—there is in fact no destination, only impassible pathways, all generative multiplicity without end, the sleights of the word-system that reside elusively on the shallow and slippery pages of the text. "Messy rather than neat, plural rather than singular, mannered and oblique rather than straightforward, it prefers the complications of the everyday and the found to the simplicities of the heroic," Hoover opines of postmodernist poetics. "Its tongue is seriously in its cheek. It is all styles rather than one."[156] Such strings of binaries like Hoover's more glaring conceptual contradictions very quickly reveal their collective and fundamental simplifications—nothing in the multiplicity of styles and voices in contemporary poetry is this neat. Instead, one must strive to be as genuinely skeptical as the ever-rigorous Simone Weil. The problem with claiming postmodernism exemplifies all styles rather than one is that it is the equivalent of saying that, essentially, postmodernist poetry is just this one thing—a pastiche of all possible ways of making poems—which of course is one kind of writing, not all. Sadly, Hoover misses his own point about pluralism and multiplicity.

He is right, however, that mannerism spans the stylistic effects of much postmodernist poetry. By mannered I assume he means a highly self-conscious heightening of stylistic effect, a de-naturalizing of the poem's voice (as if there could be a stable voice, given postmodernism's assumptions), language, and any engagement with the world, however self-referential. Perhaps Hoover is suggesting a stylization roughly akin to the overblown gestures of the 17th-century Mannerists, or of the jarringly garish use of color in Fauvist painting early in the 20th century, or the intentionally harsh, expressively garish anti-art of a Basquiat. In the 1970s, mannerism had become associated with "a mock, naïve teenage sort of detachment" that produced "fey," "daffy," "idiosyncratic" poems often allied with "received ideas."[157] This was the poetry of the so-called "deep image," a mannerism in the "use of image,"[158] and not the kind of "daffiness" one might find in postmodernism, which by definition shuns depth for surface. Still, there is something prescient in the characterization of "deep image" mannerism that feels relevant to the kind of poetry that repeats well-worn gestures, all the while adhering to a doctrinaire need to level depth to a play of surfaces.

Yet, though all roads appear to lead to endless digression in the multifarious self-enclosures of nominalist poetry, some poems in the postmodern mode follow their paths with great felt urgency, even if that urgency is "tongue in cheek." Here is the opening of John Ashbery's "The Other Tradition," which Paul Hoover wisely included in his anthology:

They all came, some wore sentiments

Emblazoned on T-shirts, proclaiming the lateness
Of the hour, and indeed the sun slanted its rays
Through branches of Norfolk Island pine as though
In a fuzz of dust under trees when it is drizzling:
The endless games of Scrabble, the boosters,
The celebrated omelette au Chantal, and through it
The roar of time plunging unchecked through the sluices
Of the days, dragging every sexual moment of it
Past the lenses: the end of something.[159]

Ashbery's poem brilliantly celebrates the "everyday over the heroic" and moves with characteristic vitality and speed from T-shirts to Norfolk Island pines to an omelet. Yet we feel confident that the poem is moving somewhere, and we feel it in the rhythms—rather traditional rhythms it turns out—carried along by Ashbery's five/six-stress line with its vaguely iambic backbeat. Where are we heading through this first long sentence? To "the roar of time plunging," to "the end of something." Far from skimming the reader across the surface, Ashbery's "new model of consciousness" deliberately carries us into the territory of ultimate questions, which is where great poems should carry us—into those heights and depths, that plunging up or down or both. Of course, the poem does not end here, but keeps us moving on its current of finely calculated perceptions and details—materializations as out of a dream of the past where a "you" appears. Is it an old lover—a stand-in for the reader? And there are troubadours! And what follows is the plunge into memory and night where the addressee speaks "like a megaphone," "not hearing or caring" in a scene that slyly echoes Stevens's "The Idea of Order at Key West." Ashbery's is not a song sung beyond the genius of the sea; rather his is speech that memorializes the evanescence of things that "have so much trouble remembering, when you're forgetting," and so "rescues them at last, as a star absorbs the night."

One wonders what Hoover is thinking when he opposes postmodernist poetry's openness to traditional poetry's closure, for "The Other Tradition" ends with extraordinary closure, the kind of explosively surprising closure that inverts and shatters brilliantly our expectations. The action of forgetting is simultaneously a saving action, as though the mind of the one remembering verged onto the edge of consciousness itself. At the end of the mind, that space beyond Stevens's "bronze décor" where language cannot venture, there is presence—the star absorbing the night—rather than absence. The star is a stock figure in traditional poetry, a long called-upon mannerism, yet Ashbery revitalizes the mannered gesture here in an extraordinary way. Whatever "continuous present," whatever mystical reality Gertrude Stein sought to flatten into her writing *is* here, but it is not in the poem as mere surface modeling—a star is a star is a star. Instead, that reality exists just beyond the edge of the poem, and despite postmodernist convention it is that realty, its height and depth and gravity, to which the poem points and of which the poem ultimately partakes. But if there is no pointing to some "beyond" outside the system, as Bernstein declares, then there is no reason to make the gesture at all.

In "The One Thing That Can Save America," Ashbery declares: "It is the humps and trials / That tell us whether we shall be known / And whether our fate can be exemplary, like a star. / All the rest is waiting."[160] Again, the figure of a star presides. Here, again, Ashbery's use of the star figure proves the inaccuracy of Hoover's forced opposition between the heroic and the everyday. The poem begins with the question "Is anything central?" It is an essential and enduring question, at once following on and antecedent to whether any center can indeed hold. Perhaps the center cannot, and there is no center, or perhaps everything is central, nothing peripheral, all potentially worthy of regard. In any case, Ashbery's best poems are not wholly "de-centered." If such poems are rooted in nominalism, they are not rooted in the manner in which a received idea is simply assumed and enacted. Rather, Ashbery's best poems take the proverbial postmodern condition as the given challenge vitally as a point of departure, drawing as urgently from tradition as from the avant-garde. That is how they give the lie to the idea that tradition and experimentation are somehow mutually exclusive. Ashbery's work at its best, of course, far exceeds the achievement of Ashbery's oppressively mannered poems, poems written as though the postmodernist vision required some new exemplification. In that vein, here is the first stanza of "Working Overtime:"

Where is Rumplestiltskin when we need him?

The glass is low,
the bard, weatherwise, who wrote
the grand old ballad of "Sir Patrick,"
comes on all queer.
Do you hear what's happening outside?[61]

"Working Overtime" reads like any other dissociative, elliptical poem produced by any one of many poets writing nearly unconsciously in the mode of the Zeitgeist—Ashbery's "fleas," as Yeats might call them, all daffy, skittery surface wit and non-sequitur. Even the allusion to "The Ballad of Sir Patrick Spens" feels forced, clever, unnecessary. Do we hear what is happening outside? No reason to go there. The sheer volume of Ashbery's production—or is it his process—warrants that there will be many lesser poems, the way artists of the kind Ashbery has reviewed for decades produce innumerable variations on the same theme. His first thirty years of published work is collected in a Library of America volume that culminates in 1986, with thirty years to go and more for the next installment. His best poems, and there are a significant number, exhibit the kind of decorative intensity in language that Matisse's work accomplished with paint and collage, a revelation not of the world of eternal things but nonetheless of intense beauty—beauty that by its nature, however mannered, points to an amplitude from which the brilliant surface gains its import and necessity.

Without detailed reference to Ashbery's epoch-defining work, Louise Glück, in her essay "On Mannerism," entertains certain components and dangers of the kind of art that rides entirely on appearances—rides as it were along the mannered surfaces in a way that infers gravity and intelligence that is actually missing from the poems. Such poems, she suggests, assume it is "less crucial to think than to appear to think, to be beheld thinking."[162] Glück's actual concern is with those that have great intellectual daring and urgency but which eschew surface difficulty. One might well cite her own work, or that of her contemporary Ellen Bryant Voigt, or any number of other contemporary American poets who do not comfortably fit within the program of "postmodernism" but who exemplify deep engagement with our "postmodern" time. In a useful phrase that summarizes many of the effects of the standard "postmodernist," "skittery," "elliptical," "experimental" poem, Glück identifies "strategies of incompleteness." These include repetition, accumulation, invocation of the void through ellipsis, dash, non-sequitur, skidding associations, and so on. All of these strategies are applicable to any poem, of course, though the issue is effectiveness, the liberation into the poem of thought and emotion truly and duly engaged with the matter of being. The point she makes is that in mannered poems "the charged moment is always charged in the same way."[163] "How much looseness, or omission, or non-relation is exciting," she asks, "and when do these devices become problematic or, worse, mannered?" It is exactly the right question, as apropos to the point as asking when or how a poem's formalism can become a product-driven exercise rather than a formal decision expressively necessary to a poem's material. What we find here, too, is mannerism: the empty performance of an idea programmed into the poem as it were rather than discovered—discovery, which is the real process that renders an accomplished poem its own experiment in language.

One notable example of the programmed poem—programmed because it obviously intends to advance the theory of poetry behind Language poetry—is Charles Bernstein's "Thank You for Saying Thank You." Here is how it opens:

This is a totally
accessible poem.
There is nothing
in this poem
that is in any
way difficult
to understand.
All the words
are simple &
to the point.
There are no new
Concepts, no
Theories, no
ideas to confuse
you . . . .[164]

Bernstein's poem proceeds for ninety lines in just this vein, creating what he understands to be a generic send up of the "mainstream" poem, or at least the ontological and epistemological skeleton of such poems. To accentuate the irony, Bernstein's poems ends: "It's / real," where the word "real" defines what the "word-system" cannot touch—reality—since whatever is real is so only within language's inescapable net. Perhaps I am misreading the poem, however, since near its end it declares itself "committed / to poetry as a / popular form, like kite / flying and fly fishing," which would suggest an idea of poetry antithetical to the ultra-theorized agenda of the Language poets, and would suggest through the simile of the kite something like a world out there that is not wholly confined to the word-system. On the other hand, the poem "Likeness" begins "the heart is like the heart / the head is like the head / the motion is like the motion / the lips are like the lips / the ocean is like the ocean / the fate is like the fate,"[165] and continues on accordingly, likening things to themselves—a negation of the category of likeness through the ironically syllogistic deployment of simile in the poem. "Likeness" goes on for several pages. Together, these poems constitute clever exercises intended to bang home the theoretical point, the same noted earlier: "the giveness of language is the giveness of the world." There is no *relation* of language to the world or vice versa—the heart is like the heart, it is not like another thing. Or does Bernstein mean that the letters h=e=a=r=t, that nominalist compendium of atomized signs, are only like the bodily organ, the center of something? Or does he mean that h=e=a=r=t is merely something we agree refers to reality by convention alone, though the atomized letters forming the word bear no substantive relation *through* language (as opposed to *in* language) to a world? What of the poet, then, according to the strict postmodernist believer? Here is the opening of "Warrant":

> I warrant that this
> poem is entirely my
> own work and that
> the underlying ideas,
> concepts, and make-up

of the poem have not
been taken from any
other source or any
other poem but rather
originate with this poem . . . .[166]

The move in these three poems is always the same—the manner of a manner—and the joke wears exceedingly thin. One thinks of the late Andy Kaufmann's painfully repetitive comedic routines, how he would intentionally frustrate the audience's expectations, coming out dressed as Elvis and lip-syncing the refrain from the Mighty Mouse cartoon—"Here I come to save the day!" "Warrant," like a number of Bernstein's poems, is antagonistic in just this way, while remaining wedded to theory as much as the business of poetry, situated as it is amidst vying schools of practice. Such poetry is a kind of entertainment, as Jack Spicer said it should be, but entertainment reserved for the few who pay for access to the club.

By contrast, here are the same intellectual concerns directed outward and fueled by genuine feeling in the first stanza of "Castor Oil," written for Bernstein's late daughter Emma, dead by suicide:

I went looking for my soul
In the song of a minor bird
But I could not find it there
Only the shadow of my thinking.[167]

These are moving lines, traditionally rendered by this poet for whom tradition is nearly anathema, communicating the bitterness of our seemingly soul-less existence. It does not indulge in a mannered exultation of linguistic parody. In his subsequent book, *Recalculating*, the poem "This is the Last Day of the Rest of Your Life 'Til Now" begins "I was the luckiest of fathers in the world / before I was the unluckiest."[168] Such poems reveal a poet far less driven by poetic and theoretical ideology and far more responsive to life, by which I mean also death, which inevitably calls all our conceptual agendas up short and renders any mannered art hollow beneath its shallow artifice (however superficially dazzling and inventive): unless the mind and heart—the heart as heart, that quaking center—contend with a deeper emptiness below all the polished surfaces.

"Every period has its manners, its signatures and, by extension, its limitations and blindness," Glück muses, "and it is particularly difficult, from the inside, to recognize such characteristics: omnipresence makes them invisible."[169] Mannerism happens when a genuine poetic signature atrophies into an empty gesture. Such work, one believes and hopes, finally becomes expendable over time, that only "the best" of the "most characteristic" within a period carries over into the forefront of literary history. "Postmodernist American Poetry" as defined by Paul Hoover in two impressively capacious anthologies positively pursues and self-consciously proclaims the centrality of mannerism under the directive that language, poetry, and reality have no place for the genuine, to adapt Marianne Moore's well-worn phrase.

If the culture of our period were able to play the old parlor game "In the Manner Of," where one person is made to leave the room while the remaining players choose an adverb to act out such that the one who had been asked to leave must guess the adverb when she returns, what might those who stayed behind in the room enact had they chosen the adverb "postmodernly," if such a word existed? If the players were some of the more than one hundred poets included in Hoover's most recent iteration of his anthology, some would act out the reigning period style with close adherence to the philosophical agenda signified by the adverb—poetry as non-sequitur, as endless repetition, as continuous present spatially represented on the page, as language game, as wallpaper. One, were one so inclined, could identify which poets most fully adhere to the tenets underlying the nominalist poem. I would suggest that these poems and poets are least likely to stand the test of time according to what we know of what endures across times and cultures. The work of other poets like Charles Olson, Denise Levertov, Kenneth Koch, Frank O'Hara, Allen Ginsburg, Robert Creeley, John Ashbery, Gary Snyder, Amiri Baraka, Fanny Howe, Jorie Graham, and many others would in no way conform to some ideologically distinct and univocal postmodernism—some presiding and defining nominalism of "the word-system." One might ask in turn: Why no Jean Valentine or Heather McHugh in the anthology, to name only two well-established contemporaries? Both invite non-sequitur and plenty of dazzling language play, though albeit to more traditionally compelling ends. The boundaries of Hoover's anthology appear shifty in a way that expresses more the politics of such anthology-making enterprises than some period and world-defining ontological condition.

In the end, there is perhaps more than a philosophical nod to Frederick Jameson and his account of late capitalism in Paul Hoover's presentation of postmodernist American poetry, with particular reference to the market. Here, Hoover affirms, are more than one hundred poets that write "postmodernly," and here are their shared presuppositions. The great carnival barker of modernist poetry, Ezra Pound, gave modernism the slogan "make it new." Ironically, he adapted the phrase from a king of the Shang Dynasty. The directive actually better translates as "renovation."[170] "Renovation" communicates a very different relationship to the past, a necessary and mutually supportive relationship rather than a wholesale rejection of what has come before. By contrast, in a recent issue of *American Poets*, Anne Waldman pays homage to Gertrude Stein's long poem *Stanzas in Mediation*, which Waldman calls "a heroic foray into uncharted poetic territory whose only subject is the act of writing itself."[171] It is an Ur text for postmodernist poetry, embodying the now thoroughly charted poetics of so much of what is au courant in contemporary poetry. "It is as though the language had assumed ownership of itself," Waldman gushes, "there is such a wonderful solipsism in this approach."[172] Solipsism is the approach, defines the approach, and sets the prime example for the approach found in so many contemporary poems of the kind likewise widely celebrated in postmodernist academia. In the guise of effacing the self into the very insubstantial stuff of language, language owned by language masquerading as mind, the poet fills the poem and the world with nothing but the self in a narcissistic pretense of self-obliteration—the selfie of a self self-obliterating. Pitched to this degree, the nominalist impulse reveals itself to be delusory. Or, as Louise Glück again warns, "narcissistic practice, no matter what ruse it appropriates, no matter what ostensible subject, is static, in that its position is self-fixed."[173] Perhaps even more egregiously, narcissism "expects us to enter into its obsession."

Obsession is not inherently bad for poets, and in fact it likely is a precondition for the making of any poem. More often than not, however, the vatic betrays its vapidity when the vatic declares in one flighty breath the poet's "wonderful solipsism" and the death of subjectivity. Given the privileged place of such in the poems of our climate, it seems apropos to quote one last time from the incomparable and pervasively imitated mater familias of postmodernist poetry and repeat the words Gertrude Stein gave to those who fell under the spell of her work: "It was not only that they liked it / It is very kind of them to like it."[174]

3. *Roadless Road*

What I have been teasing out, to uncover in an admittedly limited way, are the practical and philosophical roots of postmodernist poetry in the breakdown of Western "realism:" the belief that one can indeed extrapolate to universals from individual experience, that language and the world exist in productive relationship with each other not merely by convention but in reality. The nominalist poem in whatever manifestation assumes no such relational efficacy, or assumes in spades what Tom Sleigh has called our common "metaphysically weightless condition"[175] as a given, and therefore as the pro forma approach to making poems. The modernists faced the challenge of Western culture's metaphysical free-fall in a variety of ways. Eliot embraced religious orthodoxy to the potential exclusion of any positive cultural diversity. Stevens embraced the power of imagination as a "supreme fiction," a secular religious model of art emerging from the precious portents of our own powers. Yeats constructed his heterodox myth to inform the "personal utterance" of his poetry, and Pound made art itself a kind of highest good, a fetish benefiting the few who can crack the code that would make things new out of the unrecoverable past. Stein is the crucial figure in this last camp, for in her assumptions about writing and reality we find the blueprint for postmodernism, where one can have a very big career in the art but one cannot, in the groundless groundwork of existence, have "subjectivity." As Sleigh laments, the "I" remains "confident of its status as a linguistic entity even while the I as flesh and blood speaker whose fate is of intrinsic interest has come to an end."[176] And with the end of the "I," "the solace of formal wholeness" achieved by one stratagem or another defers to the idea that a poem must be "based on fragmentation, collage, or other nonlinear methods," all of which somehow manage presumptuously to "escape the history of styles."[177] Well aware of the epistemological and ontological predicament of contemporary poetry, Sleigh takes the strain of that predicament but does not hold with the postmodernist program: late Lowell is in his manner as associative as Ashbery, and the supposedly imperious previously presumptive "I" remains dramatically and vitally at risk without dematerializing or parading itself in a masque of parody.

In theological, historical, and sociological context, David Bentley Hart identifies the disappearance of the transcendent that so characterizes postmodernity, including Paul Hoover's encapsulating depiction of what lies behind postmodernist poetry, as something to reject. The sources of violence and cruelty are not to be found simplistically in religion but in that which precedes any cultural form—our animal natures. On the other hand, Hart ruefully observes, postmodernism indeed emerges from modernism, out of what he calls the quintessential myth of modernity: that "true freedom is the power of the will over nature—human or cosmic—and that we are at liberty to make ourselves what we wish to be."[178] This presumptuous and uncontested value ends inevitably in Nietzsche's conclusion that "only the will persists, set before the abyss of limitless possibility—or forging its way—in the dark."[179] Nietzsche's idolizing of the will typifies our postmodern condition. At the same time, ironically enough, postmodernism is "post-human" because it rejects out of hand the epistemological and ontological groundwork on which the idea of the human evolved, the idea of the "I," the person, as well as language understood as a nexus of relation to and from the world; both of these, along with the promise of transcendence on which the idea of the human finds its foundation. This post-human, Nietzschean "will" sounds contradictory—without the idea of the person, what wills?—but that is exactly the point. In Hart's postmodernist, post-human world, will operates almost as a force, freed from the core bonds of personhood, and is dehumanizing precisely because the human ground of will in the transcendent is denied. We are left with only one, univocal urgency of will—the will to power.

Interestingly, in his essay "The Noble Rider and the Sound of Words," Wallace Stevens anticipates our "post-human" world within an aesthetic rather than theological context when he reflects, "All the great things have been denied and we live in an intricacy of new and local mythologies, political, economic, poetic, which are asserted with an ever-larger incoherence. This is accompanied by an absence of any authority except force, operative or imminent."[180] Stevens's grim judgment on the social, historical, and cultural conditions in which poetry finds credence pertains even more today than it did sixty years ago. The fact that Stevens is one of the great models of the new "mannerism" only renders such claims more urgently ironic—the fraught relationship between imagination and reality was not a game for Stevens but a matter of the utmost purpose and meaning. The imagination is a necessary angel, not an arbitrary elf, not the messenger of some summary existential or ontological non-sequitur. The poetry written in the name of the avant-garde, like anything conjured by rote from a set of assumptions, maintains relevance in the history of aesthetic turf wars. Yet, when the marshal metaphor embodied in the term "avant-garde" elides more egregious eventualities of will impacting the lives, and deaths, of real persons, then the relative irrelevance of art finds common ground with far graver matters. It always has. When the purely philosophical and aesthetic assumption of "the death of the subject" abuts the deaths of millions of subjects in flesh and blood due to the will to power, then the favors of a postmodernist "Ethernity" over a traditional "Eternity" come to sound wildly utopian, however well-intended they appear to be with their pretense of saving us from the old brutalities, gods, empires, and the various insidious oppressions of "the metaphysical."

There are two basic confusions underlying the postmodernist poetic program, and by the postmodernist poetic program I do not mean tout corps all "experimental" or avant-garde poets, some of whom have written marvelous individual poems. All great poems are experimental—they at once create a world and enable us to see the world anew. I mean instead to take issue with the nominalist reductionism that informs the basis for the poetics so clearly articulated by Paul Hoover. As William Lynch explains, once "the whole action and division of the sensible world" has been "obliterated," and language and reality set apart by an impassible gulf, then somehow the poem itself becomes a way "to get a hold of . . . a world of pure being."[181] The first confusion is to make poetry the inverse of some static Eternity, or a static "Ethernity." Here, again, we find Stein's "continuous present." One would presume this Ethernity to be ethereal, but the claim rests on a foundation of radical materialism, and so Stein's practice, like that of many who follow after her resides in an idea of art as inaction. "Generally speaking," she quips, "anybody is more interesting doing nothing than doing something."[182] Stein's celebration of inaction likewise supports her conception of poetry as concerned exclusively with the noun— verbs need not apply.[183] For Stein, poetry is fundamentally anti-dramatic, which is diametrically opposed to Frost's view that any piece of writing is only as good as it is dramatic. Yet, there is good reason to believe that action is, in Frost's words, "the soul of the literary imagination in all its scope and forms, and that metaphor either springs out of action as one of its finest fruits, or is itself one of its many forms."[184] It is a concept to which Owen Barfield wholly adheres when he asks, "What is absolutely necessary for the present existence of poetry?" He answers: "the real presence of movement."[185] Movement, by definition, assumes relation—relation manifest in language and in reality, requiring the real presence of both, as necessary as any sacrament. Literary imagination is an action of consciousness; without its action there is no art, indeed there is no reality, at least in any humanly conceivable terms.

This brings us to the second confusion, which is nothing less than a muddle about "the metaphysical structure of reality itself."[186] "Meaning" has never been conceived as residing in some centrally accessible "metaphysical" storehouse from which it is packaged and parceled and distributed. Such an Eternity would be as static as the aforementioned Ethernity, the two existing at opposite ontological and epistemological poles: conceptual matter and antimatter canceling each other out. What William Lynch calls "the equivocal" view of reality—everything atomized and running divergently from everything else—is nothing other than the nominalist conception of things that lies at the core the postmodernist reality. At its furthest reach, the equivocal collapses into its opposite, the univocal—a reductive unity that erases all difference. That is why for Hoover all styles converge into one in the endless shell game of postmodernism. By contrast, what is necessary is to envision reality as "the interpenetration of unity and multiplicity, sameness and difference, a kind of interpenetration in terms of which the two contraries become one and the same thing—but become this only because existentially they have always been it."[187] Such is "the metaphysics of analogy." In that metaphysics, reality is anything but static. Unity and sameness require multiplicity and difference because all things exist through participation *with and through each other*. We exist in a field or fields of action. When Charles Olson enjoins poets to write in the "open field," he is unknowingly calling on the fundamentals of a very long tradition of which he does not appear to be entirely aware—hence the call for revolution, to again "make it new." Interestingly, A.R. Ammons, a poet committed to the aesthetic of the "open field" regarded the ontological relationship between "the Many and the One" to be the essential question his poetry sought to address. It was for him the central mystery of reality. In his essay "A Poem is a Walk" he reflects: "the statement All is One provides for no experience of manyness, of the concrete world from which the statement derived. But a work of art creates a world both one and many, a world of definition and in-definition."[188] If Lynch and Ammons are right, then in Lynch's words "the *one* is not a dead, monotonous fact; it only becomes itself by articulating itself into many jointings and members."[189] The analogical vision of reality has been the foundation of the mainline of Western metaphysics since at least the 4th century of the Common Era, though one could trace strands of it much earlier in the cultures of the West—Plato's metaxu. Rather than a static straw man Eternity, the analogical vision depends and builds on adaptation, renewal, improvisation, revision, and—to make itself new—ongoing renovation in the middle ground of existence.

Essential likewise to analogical metaphysics is the inherently positive valuation of language and its relationship to material reality. The analogical is anything but world denying, despite the fact that so often western culture and its religious institutions have failed miserably to live up to the affirming implications of the idea. If the analogical vision of reality has deep roots in human culture and consciousness, then so too does the antithetical world-denying impulse. It is possible to see the roots of so pervasive a negation of the human in Greek and Roman culture, well before the advent of nominalism. That negation resides for David Bentley Hart in the "glorious sadness" of both the tragic vision of ancient Greece and Rome's "theatre of cruelty" founded as it is on the imposition of power, the exploitation of the weak.[190] Nonetheless, great art flowered there too, as always, and as an enduring expression of a human quest for meaning and not merely a product of culture.

In the alternative Gnostic Christianities of the first five centuries of the Common Era, the world-denying spirit also found vigorous advocacy and practice. There were many varieties of Gnostic sects, from Valentinianism to Marcionism to Manicheism. Collectively, they exerted a useful negative pressure that enabled orthodox Christianity to gain communal, creedal, structural, and cultural definition and dominance. In our postmodern era, we tend to favor the heterodox, the syncretistic, the belief that all beliefs or no belief are equally true since belief, like all of reality, is nothing more than a cultural construction harboring no essential truth. Yet, had Marcion prevailed over orthodox advocates Irenaeus and Tertullian, the Hebrew Bible (to cite just one example) would not have been incorporated into the Christian faith. Marcion and his followers believed "the Old Testament God" to be a false god, the god of this world, a demiurge deluding all but the elite few. The rest will forever be mired in materiality. Anti-Semitism has been a cultural virus and vicious scourge throughout history. How much worse would things have been had the God of the Jewish people been deemed a false god, an evil god, and not the same God as the One God of the dominant Christian religion? Would Judaism have survived? More to the point, these two principal concepts— that the visible cosmos was ruled by Darkness (in the form of false gods, principalities, powers, archons, and the like) resistant to the true immaterial God, and that escape from this world is made only by an elite who obtain secret knowledge, gnosis—governed all forms of Gnosticism regardless of particular differences in doctrine.

What has Gnosticism to do with postmodernism and postmodernist poetry? Many have already recognized the parallel nature of our own time to the cultural ferment of two thousand years ago—that "Age of Anxiety," as W.H. Auden's friend, the historian E.R. Dodds, called it.[191] If postmodernity constitutes a "post-human" era, then our leveling of the cosmos to a universe defined by materialism in which language and reality are mutually divested from each other transports us to a belated Gnostic cosmos without exit. Ours, too, is a universe governed by force in which individuals and nations are bound to pit their wills against each other. There is a second parallel that makes Gnosticism's inherent elitism prescient and relevant for postmodernist aesthetics. "Like circles of artists today," Elaine Pagels writes, "Gnostics considered original creative invention to be the mark of anyone who becomes spiritually alive."[192] Art, in short, must be avant-garde, revolutionary in the belated and self-contradictory meaning of the word—not a return to beginnings for renewal but an obliteration of the old under the rubric of "original creative invention." Postmodernism at its core is world-denying, for it is a vision of the world founded on the impossibility of relation, of action. That is its paradox. Within its nexus, all actions, including aesthetic action, mirror and reiterate the presiding chaos. Is the best to be done nothing more than parody and wallpaper, since the age of "the literary gem" is now forever passé?[193] Samuel Beckett's genius, by way of one keen example, was too existentially and humanly sensitive even at his grimmest to succumb to the full implications of the postmodernist vision, though like Stein he anticipates our time. Yet unlike Stein, Beckett's art rises above our moment and his own with a kind of majestic deprivation, the analogical vision alive in homeless clowns and talking heads enduring in their despair. Such an art is anything but elitist. Beckett's minimalism is maximally embracing rather than mannerist—a mannerism minimal in its ambitions and maximal in its claims. On the contrary, Beckett's world resonates profoundly with Weil's understanding of affliction, so much so that *Waiting for Godot*, his most representative work, literally encodes Weil's *Waiting for God* in its title.

Though both appear world-negating in their effective vision of reality, there remains a drastic existential difference between the claims of Gnosticism and the claims of postmodernism. In Valentinus's version of the quest for gnosis, the searcher's path begins with the recognition of *kakia*, the Greek word for illness, though illness of this variety is more like Sartre's existential "nausea"—a feeling part and parcel of the material conditions of being rather than of mere spiritual disaffection. The journey begins with the Gnostic recognition that "all materiality was formed from three experiences [or, sufferings]: terror, pain, and confusion [*aporia*; literally 'roadlessness,' not knowing where to go]."[194] Such roadlessness is actually Dantean: "Midway through the journey of our life, I found / myself in a dark wood, for I had strayed / from the straight pathway to this tangled ground."[195] The difference between Valentinus and the Florentine poet some thirteen hundred years later is that Dante believed bodily existence and spiritual life found communion in the Incarnation. He believed in an analogical universe. For Valentinus, whatever signs might be present in the world, the world itself is materially and irreparably fallen—one follows Christ to escape it, which is why in Gnostic Christology the figure of Christ is understood as a phantom displaying the guise of material existence and not a flesh and blood human being who is still of one substance with the divine nature.

Aporia, roadlessness, is a common word used to describe the postmodern condition. The difference is that in postmodernism aporia ceases to be just an existential condition and mutates into a condition of language and being. It becomes univocal, inescapable. What was heresy for orthodox Christians in the alternative Christianities of the first few centuries of the Common Era attunes itself to postmodernism's heterodox, "equivocal," orthodoxy. The word *heresy*, like aporia, comes from the Greek and means "to choose." From the orthodox perspective, the heretic "chooses" to embrace false opinions or beliefs.[196] The postmodernist embraces aesthetic heresy, happily transgressing established boundaries. Or as Paul Hoover has outlined, the postmodernist poet falls under the rubric of a well-formed paradigm of reality that the poems reiterate in their aesthetic choices. Collectively those choices reflect "a zeitgeist." If not exactly a belated version of Gnosticism, postmodernism proclaims the material, epistemological, and ontological reality of the aporia, of roadlessness—the pathless path of art as an endless errancy accruing to no end, process without purpose, and all inherently siphoned of value.

There are a great many practitioners of postmodernist American poetry and one could trace some of the proclivities I have tried to outline in a great many poems—the mannerisms of the postmodernist poet happily and self-confidently heretical, self-thrilled with choices to transgress for the sake of transgression. Here, by way of example, is the first section of Michael Dickman's "Emily Dickinson to the Rescue" from his James Laughlin Award-winning book, *Flies*:

> Standing in her house today all I could think of was whether she took a shit every morning
>
> or ever fucked anybody
> or ever fucked
> herself
>
> God's poet
> singing herself to sleep
>
> You want these sorts of things for people
>
> Bodies and
> the earth
> and
>
> the earth inside
>
> Instead of white
> nightgowns and terrifying
> letters[197]

In a recent issue of *American Poet*, one of the judges for the award praises Dickman's work for its "Kafkaesque hilarity," and even his punctuation, which the judge believes functions like Dickinson's dashes (with a smattering of Frank Bidart thrown in for good measure). The outsized comparisons to Kafka and Dickinson are hard to take seriously, unless Kafka was an adolescent who watched too many zombie movies and Dickinson was more inclined to record her bowel movements, her inclination toward masturbation, and her back-room liaisons with her father's hunky Irish gardeners. Dickman's poem begins with the willfully "shocking" thought of Emily Dickinson voiding herself instead of facing the Void, as she does so often, and moves on from there "bravely" to undo our image of "God's poet" by immersing her ever more deeply into the earthly mire. In this instance, that mire is more expressive of the poet's immature psyche than of any vital relation to Dickinson. The poem exemplifies the kind of knee-jerk ironic style and shock value that has become not only commonplace but feted with awards.

Irony as a willed style offers from poet Ellen Bryant Voigt's perspective only "cleverness" rather than a genuinely discrepant angle. Genuine irony has the power to shock and reveal discrepant truths—like slaves building the Capitol of the United States of America.[198] "Worse," Voigt strikes to the heart of the matter, "poets may doubt the possibility of any sort of meaning in the world, and content themselves with an allegedly mimetic representation of disparate, even random fragments of observation and experience."[199] From this vantage, a poem like "Emily Dickinson to the Rescue" imposes the poet's presumptuous stance like someone scratching witticisms on a bathroom stall. In this vein, toward the end of his poem "An Offering" Dickman declares "I have made so many mistakes that I must wake all the Lords up / early so we can get a head start on cleaning some of this shit up." Clearly shit carries substantial figurative weight in Dickman's poetry. Here he calls on the "Lords"—his sister, grandma, grandpa, the boss—the way a latter-day Gnostic faced with the aporia of life might call on the archons of material reality to allow him to pass through. There is no passing through, or out, except in the self-evident manner of language voiding itself into the unavoidable void that is reality and the poem—voided, one must admit, with considerable self-congratulation onto the page for our delectation. The poet carries his poem into the public sphere like a child in potty training and hands over the fresh stool: "See what I made."

It could be argued that Michael Dickman's "Emily Dickinson to the Rescue" and "An Offering" are poems that do intend to mean, that happily or unhappily express subjectivity, and therefore do not conform to any doctrinaire version of postmodernism. On the other hand, Dickman's poems do express postmodernism's zeitgeist. They appear motivated primarily to level hierarchies and to shock. "Emily Dickinson to the Rescue" does not evoke the greatness of its subject. The height and depth of Dickinson's vision flattens to the lowest conceivable denominator—material existence exemplified by shitting and fucking. All of which is necessary, but not necessarily all. Both the aesthetic and the ontological vision exemplified in Dickinson's poems stand in starkest contrast to Dickinson's own work, and they affirm with Weil that art ultimately "is an attempt to transport into a limited quantity of matter. . . an image of the infinite beauty of the entire universe."[200] With a radical faith that would win her few supporters in contemporary academic life, Weil concludes: "God has inspired every first-rate work of art, though its subject may be utterly and entirely secular."[201] So assured and exalted a view of art's connection to the divine has been largely expunged from contemporary aesthetics, governed as it has become by a metaphysical materialism.

Beyond leveling hierarchies, Dickman's work manifests some of the characteristics of what Stephanie Burt calls "Elliptical School" of poets. "Look for a persona and a world, not for an argument or a plot," Burt exhorts. The persona of Dickman's poems is fairly consistent and pervasive in the zeitgeist. It is more attitude, as Tony Hoagland has observed, than an outright persona,[202] a kind of blithely unyielding and doggedly adolescent weltschmertz that takes nothing seriously except its own posture, its manner of disaffection. When emotion finds expression in such poems it is usually melodramatic. More to the core is the idea that the poems of the zeitgeist "resemble games whose rules you can learn,"[203] the hinting, the punning, the perpetual swerving away from sense, the particulate concentrations that forestall any sense of the whole. In his poem "Pomegranates," Charles Bernstein deliberately replaces the phrase "We can't avoid structure" with the erasure "a void structure." At bottom, or on depthless surface, we find only language without logos, without purpose or end—language and poetry revealed as an unavoidably voided structure.

Paul Ricoeur, the great philosopher of language and metaphor, would have us view matters very differently. "It is in language," Ricoeur reminds us, "that the cosmos, desire, and the imaginary reach expression; speech is always necessary if the world is to be recovered and made hierophany,"[204] literally a showing of the sacred. What language gives us rather than a void structure is "surpluses of meaning" born of language's relational capacity, its inherent "I–Thou" structure, its capacity for polysemy, for making meanings—its analogical function and essence. Metaphor reveals the quintessence of language for in metaphor we find designated "the general process by which we grasp kinship, break the distance between remote ideas, build similarities on dissimilarities" by exploiting "the tension between sameness and difference."[205] Here, again, at the core of language-making, we find Weil's conception of metaxu—of bridges. Where microcosm and macrocosm meet is in metaphor. The power of poetry, then is "not to improve communication," nor ensure the power of one singular voice over another as an imposition of will. Rather poetry's power is "to shatter and to increase our sense of reality by shattering and increasing our language."[206] Language, like reality, is metamorphosis. Or as A.R. Ammons ventured in his poem *Garbage*, the problem is not that there is no meaning but that there is so much meaning "we don't know what to do with all the meaning." That infinite surplus of meaning is precisely what postmodernism misses and to which it blinds its adherents. As the meaning embedded in the word heretic teaches us, we have to choose, and one hopes more poets will choose the road that blazes a path through roadlessness back to the co-inherence, to the communion, of language and reality. The poet who decides to make this choice, alas it appears more and more, will be an outlier among the throng of fractious wallpaper hangers all passing by.

4. *Brand*

Brightly vested in their loose smocks, the ebullient troop sways rhythmically onto the floor, their gold drums strapped before them around their waists. The drummers' arms move in unison, felt mallets the size of tennis balls pound confidently, the great percussive rush amplifies to fill the arena with aplomb and applause. Grooversity is in the building. Now the troop splits in two to navigate the aisles separating hundreds of empty chairs where, just weeks earlier, the hockey rink would await its intrepid skaters. They align themselves in front of the raised dais with its microphones and teleprompters as the leader raises his arms to the cheering crowd of thousands. Along the digital rim below the rafters the College's name flashes and glows, white letters, a bright purple band. Four massive screens will simulcast the ceremony; will broadcast pre-recorded encouragement from a pithy alum array happy to urge the graduates onward to success, to developing and advancing their personal brands. Though if one closed one's eyes, all this could be the hoopla of some ancient ritual, the opening celebration of games held between city states, or, today, a long-promoted boxing match—Las Vegas, its neon dazzle and panache. From a channel under the stands the faculty process, all mortarboards and tams and medieval gowns, the occasional bare head—some grooving awkwardly to the drums, some in time, most marching dutifully—but for the one in the black baseball cap, no team insignia, taking in the scene. Let's call that one the heretic poet. There, with the platform party, is another poet, the commencement speaker, engaging, funny, self-deprecating, greatly popular. He will have the graduates and their families laughing and clapping, even the faculty nodding in appreciation for the light touch with its hint of profundity, the nods to the masters. One suspects even the student graduating with the self-designed major "Performance Poetry Transforming the World" will find his remarks entertaining.

The scene I have sketched portrays accurately the commencement exercises held at a notable American college dedicated in its niche fashion to the study of communications and the arts, and means to highlight for the moment a broader perspective on the situation of poetry now relative to the roadless road of postmodernist practice. Perhaps, like the split rows of chairs demarking separate areas within the student population, it means to suggest pathways or an arrangement of crossroads (if not bridges) between and among approaches, sensibilities, disciplines. On the other hand, it might be best not to overwork the conceit. Let's say there are two principal figures here, ignoring for the time being our heretic poet with his incongruous hat amidst the sea of floating tams and mortarboards. Let's say the principal figure for the moment is our affably and ruefully articulate commencement speaker, and let's say that speaker is Billy Collins— "Literary Lion," winner of many noteworthy awards, former poet laureate of the United States, and bestselling author of numerous poetry collections. Usually one might consider the phrase "popular poet" an oxymoron, but not in the case of Billy Collins. What Charles Bernstein ironically evokes in his poem "Thank You for Saying Thank You," Billy Collins embodies genuinely, for Collins really is "committed / to poetry as a / popular form, like kite / flying and fly fishing." At the antipodes to postmodernist practice resides the work of popular poetry, the kind of poetry that looks at the world with a wry attentiveness and easefully literate intelligence, inviting the audience to sail with the poet around the room, to paraphrase the title of Collins's selected poems. Collins has become that most unlikely of oxymorons—a bestselling poet. He is effectively, by poetry standards, his own brand.

In the case of "Taking Off Emily Dickinson's Clothes," one of his many widely known poems, Collins offers an affectionate take on one of the language's most formidably brilliant poets whose brand—if one can call her unlikely canonicity a brand—appeals perhaps to a somewhat different readership. Here is the opening:

> First, her tippet made of tulle,
> easily lifted off her shoulders and laid
> on the back of a wooden chair.
>
> And her bonnet,
> the bow undone with a light forward pull . . . .[207]

One can see more or less immediately where the poem is going and how the poet means to bring us there. If we attune ourselves to the clever first line, we know the poem invites us into its fantasy of unclothing the Maid of Amherst through a series of allusions to her own poems and the Spartan circumstances of her life, riffs lightly touched and re-touched as Collins's lines advance easefully down the page. The goal is not to disrupt or jar—certainly not to shock with the sophomoric glee of Matthew Dickman's "Emily Dickinson to the Rescue." Nor is it to be "wallpaper." Nor, however, does it seek to challenge the reader the way Dickinson inevitably does by encountering the nakedness of being at its psychic core through the metaphorical richness and conscious probity of her hymn-like stanzas. The goal is to orchestrate a narrative of pleasantly surprising incongruity so entertainingly that the reader hardly realizes the poet is deftly demythologizing his formidable subject and simultaneously seducing the reader to join him in his affectionate voyeurism. The poem is fancifully engaging, and many a reader would be bound to fancy it.

Not to be outdone, Collins has his own flair for metaphor and simile—
his hands part the fabric of Dickinson's white dress "like a swimmer's dividing
water," until in the poem's fourth stanza the dress puddles at her feet and he
finally sails "toward the iceberg of her nakedness." There are effortless tonal
modulations as well: "The complexity of women's undergarments / in 19th
century America / is not to be waved off . . . ." Thus, the poet proceeds "like
a polar explorer" through the clips and clasps and moorings and whalebone
stays, until the poem turns "postmodernly" self-reflexive: "Later, I wrote in a
notebook / it was like riding a swan into the night, / but, of course, I cannot
tell you everything . . . ." What the poet does tells us is a series of further riffs
on Dickinson's own poems, "how there were sudden dashes whenever we
spoke," allusions to Death's carriage that stopped for her, the fly buzzing at the
windowpane, the plank in reason that breaks before she drops down and down,
hitting a world at every plunge before she finishes knowing.

From the vantage of inventive conception, witty playfulness, and an
engagingly accessible tone, "Taking Off Emily Dickinson's Clothes" sails
appealing through the wry turns of its tryst, whether kite-like in Bernstein's
ironic formula or merely around the rooms of its stanzas. Even the un-
Dickensian allusion to Yeats's "Leda and the Swan"—"like riding a swan into
the night"—offers a sly inversion of the Irish poet's mythological critique. From
another vantage, the poem could be seen as something artfully akin to mellow
jazz. The poem puts one at ease, but does it nudge the reader by indirection or
subliminally into Dickinson's own spiritual urgency, the spiritual nakedness at
the core of her poems? One must say no. To push a bit harder, what does it do to
our appreciation of Emily Dickinson to portray her as a sexually frigid spinster?
One does not need to read very deeply into the vast Dickinson oeuvre to feel
the spiritual passion that lets itself loose physically with a vital urgency—"Wild
Nights, Wild Nights"—as well as the most passionate sadness. Such poems are
as far from frigid as anything could be: "I cannot live with you / It would be
Life / And Life is over there / Upon the Shelf . . . ."[208] In contrast, this fancifully
frigid Emily Dickinson is something other than the demythologized figure of
immense genius. For all his wit and ingenuity, the poem feels something closer
to a pastel portrait, the popularly branded idea of Emily Dickinson, and not the

extraordinary mind and heart we discover in the poems.

Another kind of contemporary popular poem, related in formal ease to "Taking Off Emily Dickinson's Clothes," offers less by way of wit and ingenuity and more by way of plangent affirmations. At the upper echelon of this brand of populist poetry one finds the work of the late Mary Oliver. Oliver won the Pulitzer Prize for *American Primitive* some thirty-five years ago, which was the height of her accomplishment in the art. Like Billy Collins, she is one of the most popular of American poets and as such a staple on Poetry in Motion, that most concerted, celebrated, and civic-minded effort to bring poetry to the widest possible audience. Oliver, within the limited frame of late capitalist American poetry, has become a brand. Among people who find themselves drawn to "accessible poetry," her work has the quality called "being relatable." By way of example, Oliver's "An Old Story" appeared recently on the Boston T. It begins with the convergence of sleep and spring along with the poet waking "in the valley of midnight" to a quietly momentous revelation:

> My heart says, what you thought you had you do not have.
> My body says, will this pounding ever stop?
>
> My heart says, there, there, be a good student.
> My body says, let me up and out, I want to fondle
> those soft white flowers, open in the night.[209]

Oliver's poem aims to appeal to some common, one might say generic, emotional core, and it does so by trading in stock figures—"valley of midnight"—and the consolations of an easy transcendentalism. This nighttime dialogue of heart and body has little of the necessary urgency of a dialogue of self and soul, of the kind Yeats demanded of himself and his readership, or Oliver's own best work. The poem "fondles" the reader with a soft universalism, a silken blurrily focused univocal portrait the poet presumes we all must share. It is after all an Old Story, rendered now without any drama of consciousness. We are not all that terribly far from Rupi Kaur, the most popular of contemporary poets, a veritable Instagram phenomenon. Here is one of her faux Rumi verities: "he isn't coming back / whispered my head / he has to / sobbed my heart."[210]

To paraphrase Dorothy upon her arrival in Oz, I think we're not in poetry anymore; though to say as much is to be considered elitist or condescending in the current milieu. Others have parlayed celebrity into the moniker of poet— Art Garfunkle, Suzanne Somers, Richard Thomas, Leonard Nimoy—but other than Rod McKuen it is hard to recollect a "poet" parlaying their "art" into celebrity of this magnitude. Kaur's brand extends to millions. Such is the leveling effect of the postmodern in its popular form—and the shrewdness of this "artist" to ride with aesthetic abandon the flood-tide of social media. Against such effluvia there are the likes, again, of Yeats, and Yeats's riveting dialogue between Self and Soul, of which Self has the final say:

> I am content to follow to its source
> Every event in action or in thought;
> Measure the lot; forgive myself the lot!
> When such as I cast out remorse
> So great a sweetness flows into the breast
> We must laugh and we must sing,
> We are blest by everything.
> Everything we look upon is blest.[211]

With his characteristic lighter touch, Billy Collins' work can approach this level of urgency, as at the beginning of his poem "The Afterlife": "While you are preparing for sleep, brushing your teeth, / or riffling through a magazine in bed, / the dead of the day are setting out on their journey."[212] The remainder of the poem marvelously introduces the reader to the life of the dead and their final longing to return to the living, and ends with a brilliant image for poetry itself—"the winter trees, / every branch traced with the ghost writing of snow." Likewise, Mary Oliver's work at its best, as in "Hawk," captures nature and the mind's encounter with an indelible vitality, as when the hawk rising out the meadow settles "on the small black dome / of a dead pine, / alert as an admiral, / its profile / distinguished with sideburns / the color of smoke" and it compels the poet to an overwhelming recognition: "remember / this is not something / of the red fire, this is / heaven's fistful / of death and destruction."[213] Neither of these poems, "The Afterlife" nor "Hawk," gravitate to aesthetic populism, for all their accessibility. Though each achieves in its own idiom the gravitas of genuine poetry.

Once, riding the Dublin Area Rapid Transit train—the DART—from City Center to Howth to visit Balscadden Cottage where Yeats lived for a time as a young poet, I caught sight of the indelible lines of "Sailing to Byzantium" next to an ad for Tayto Crisps. Seamus Heaney's sonnet about peeling potatoes with his mother was recently voted Ireland's favorite poem. Whatever goes by the name of "popular poetry" appears always to be a local phenomenon. On the other hand, the spoken word poet Holly McNish has surged in popularity across the United Kingdom and all of Europe. Such news would certainly hearten one of the other figures in the Commencement arena, our graduating student with the self-designed major animated by genuine commitment and idealism. Can performance poetry save the world, as they believe, or was Auden right when he said poetry makes nothing happen? Then again, is performance poetry an entirely new phenomenon in the age of social media and the Internet? As one of my best students one told me in passing, "All of the poets I most respect have Twitter accounts." Many poets do, now, have Twitter accounts, though it is hopefully if not probably true that the brand of a Twitter handle will not bring one's work to posterity, only the achievement of the work itself.

One of the real powers of performance and spoken word poetry as a type of popular poetry lies in community building—something sorely needed if Yuval Noah Harari is right, and "the local intimate community" for which we are evolutionarily wired has collapsed since the onward march of our technologically advancing postmodernity.[214] From another vantage, performance poetry turns the art of poetry *back* to its roots in ritual, or in theatre, or the mead hall. A poet such as Patricia Smith, to choose the most obvious example, means that performance for the stage need not preclude performance on the page. Yeats himself advanced in his art by writing for the stage, by grounding his fluent lyricism in dramatic speech.

Concurrent with performance poetry, what has come to be called in some circles "identity poetry"—the kind of poetry that foregrounds identification with a social or cultural group as a defining characteristic of the subject matter—has not only gained in popularity but has gained, also, an academic foothold. There are many very fine contemporary poets who might well be named—many fine young poets who inspire the likes of our idealistic graduate—and who communicate considerable political urgency. They form, perhaps, a different avant-garde than Hoover's rather academically entrenched postmodernists, as though their own brand were somehow suddenly fading from the limelight despite protestations to the contrary.

Yet, so called "identity poetry" also is not new. In aligning his work with the Irish Literary Renaissance and in fueling that Renaissance as vanguard, Yeats's poems pushed the matter of Irish identity on a recalcitrant British Empire to substantial political effect. Similarly, a poem like Adrienne Rich's "Diving into the Wreck" continues to be an aesthetic and political landmark in the advancement of women's and LGBTQ voices, and a measure for all serious practitioners of the art. Perhaps for our own socially urgent moment the great example is Gwendolyn Brooks. Her mastery of the masters in every sense, aesthetically and politically, manifests itself everywhere in her work. When she explores the virulently flawed mentality of racism and racial violence in such poems as "The Lovers of the Poor" and "A Bronzeville Mother Loiters in Mississippi, Meanwhile, a Mississippi Burns Bacon," she exposes the mindset of that virulence with consummate artistry. When at the end of "The Boy Died in my Alley" she writes, "The red floor of my alley / is a special speech to me," she at once gives voice to the voiceless and calls out those authorities who remain blind to, if not complicit with, the system. Her importance, as Elizabeth Alexander affirms, is incontestable. She has been "one of the most influential poets of the twentieth century" even as "her poems distill the very best aspects of the Modernist style with the sounds and shapes of various African-American forms and idioms."[215] Her sustaining influence and mastery is perhaps best exemplified in "The Sermon on the Warpland." With extraordinary prescience, her ars poetica affirms the ultimate significance of her identity and the identity of her people:

> Build now your Church, my brothers, sisters. Build
> never with brick or Corten nor with granite.
> Build with lithe love. With love like lion-eyes.

With love like morningrise.
With love like black, our black—
luminously indiscreet;
complete; continuous.[216]

Devoted to her community, and to a vision of love that must inevitably transcend the limits of social, historical, and cultural boundaries, Gwendolyn Brooks's work is beyond branding. As her work emerged into its late maturity she chose, in fact, the smaller community press rather than the "major" press that published her early Pulitzer Prize-winning work. In our era of poetry branding, that would be a counterintuitive decision. From the standpoint of canon, evidenced in the entire body of her work, the legacy of Gwendolyn Brooks's poetry is that she refuses to collapse standards into the obliquities of taste, to invoke Agha Shahid Ali's important distinction.[217] Rather, she expands the standards of tradition and canon without lessening them, without relegating the poet's art to the very real and at times perceived tout corps oppressions of a static, monolithic tradition. She was well aware early on, as Elizabeth Alexander reflects, of the "pressure" for black writers "to prove their literacy . . . through the mastery of European forms."[218] The well documented change heralded in her late poetry was a turning toward and an even fuller embrace of her community, though it is not a repudiation of the European tradition. Rather, it signals an enlargement and revitalization not only of the canon, but of the traditions of poetry in English, that continues today in the work of a wide variety of voices from many cultural, ethnic, and gender vantage grounds.

One might underscore this dual current of revitalization and enlargement through the equally important figure of Robert Hayden, whose Ba'ha'i faith, in concert with his poetics, placed a primacy on the unification of humanity over racial identification and the more "vernacular" practices of the Black Arts Movement of the late 1960s and 1970s. Yet, what Derik Smith calls Hayden's more traditional "writerly" aesthetic is best understood to be a dissenting voice within the Black Arts Movement and its identity-based activism, rather than an oppositional stance projected from outside.[219] Hayden's famous dressing-down by Melvin Tolson (and others in attendance) at the Fisk University Conference of 1966 set the trajectory for the narrative of Hayden's outsider status, as well as what might be viewed as the anti-performative approach to his art. Anyone who has read Hayden's magisterial poems, from the duly famous "Those Winter Sundays" to the blues-based work of "Homage to the Empress of the Blues," to the modernist collage of "Middle Passage," surely knows how "writerly" a poet Hayden is, and how formally astute. Yet, the helpful delineation "writerly" and "vernacular" may, in the end, fashion too neat a dichotomy. As the opening lines of his early poem "Electrical Storm" suggest, in Hayden's poetry the writerly does not exist in opposition to the vernacular; rather, this is a poet who masterfully negotiates between and among multiple vernaculars with the most writerly of intentions:

> God's angry with the world again
> The grey, neglected ones would say;
> He don't like ugly.
> Have mercy, Lord, they prayed,
> Seeing the lightning's
> Mene Mene Tekel . . . .[220]

These lines move from the idiomatic to a "writerly" iambic tetrameter to the street speech of his childhood Paradise Valley in Detroit to the biblical, and they do so as though effortlessly. The first line of "Those Winter Sundays" reads "Sundays too my father got up early"—hardly "writerly" if by that one means a tone notably different from plausible speech. The language is thoroughly idiomatic, the vernacular of a particular Everyman with an individual history looking back to his beginnings. Likewise, to read "Middle Passage" or "Runagate Runagate," to name but two examples, is to encounter a poet fully engaged culturally with his identity as an African-American, wholly mindful of his historical moment, keenly aware of the history of oppression so sadly formative of America (and human history more generally), and richly conversant with the many technical attributes of his singular art. Perhaps, then, it is not surprising that in his manifesto, "Counterpoise," he declares: "as writers who belong to a so-called minority we are violently opposed to having our work viewed, as the custom is, entirely in the light of sociology and politics."[221]

In this tellingly forthright sentence the word "entirely" rings out crucially at a time when a statement like "All poetry is politics" has become commonplace. Likewise, in his essay "How it Strikes a Contemporary," Hayden cautions against the tendency to confuse poetry with "therapy." "A great many people are writing poetry today," he reflects, "I do not call them poets [. . .] who are not so much concerned with art or craft as they are with achieving some emotional or psychic release."[222] The concern with art, with craft, stands crucially as Hayden's ultimate concern in poetry—the art, moreover, he regards as a form of prayer:

> Though I eschew the didactic, I admit to being a poet "with a purpose." Naturally, I want my poetry to stand primarily as poetry. But I want it to serve God and affirm and honor [humanity], however indirectly. I think of writing a poem as a prayer for understanding and perfection—indeed, as a form of worship.[223]

In light of his masterful work and his reflections on the poet's craft, it appears very likely that Robert Hayden would agree with Agha Shahid Ali's observation that not all "identity" poems are necessarily good poems, and that there are standards that mark true greatness.

"What are your standards?" Shahid Ali asks of those who would repudiate tradition out of hand. It would appear that certain contemporary poets have no way of offering a reply to this unavoidable question, and instead offer only the elision of aesthetics into politics. It is a stance, Shahid Ali believes, that can quickly become a distraction from the poet's "real work into a facilely executed sense of social justice."[224] This betrayal of the poet's work into what he calls "the programmatic" can, occasionally, lead to vitriol. Here, by way of a contemporary counter example to Hayden and Shahid Ali, is the opening of Eileen Myles's "On the Death of Robert Lowell":

> O, I don't give a shit.
> He was an old white-haired man
> Insensate beyond belief and
> Filled with much anxiety about his imagined
> Pain. Not that I know.

I hate fucking wasps.[225]

From here Eileen Myles goes on to lampoon "the old white-haired loon's" time at McLean Hospital, dismissing a poet who has written demonstrably great poems and who, like Ray Charles and James Taylor, the poet reminds us, "once rested there." "The famous, as we know, are nuts." More curse poem than elegy, Myles's "The Death of Robert Lowell" has nothing to say about making with "lithe love." It has everything to say, however inadvertently, about how blind ideology undermines the art that a poet presumes to practice with the utmost seriousness and ambition: "Take Robert Lowell. / The old white haired coot. / Fucking dead." While it is true, to an extent, as Adrienne Rich recognized, that "what really matters . . . is the poet's voice and concerns refusing to be circumscribed or colonized by tradition, the tradition being just a point of takeoff,"[226] it is equally true that a poet's personal voice should not presume denigration of another as the privilege of its right to be heard. Tradition does not inherently circumscribe a poet's voice, forcing the poet to conform to its "format." On the contrary, a poet's voice might just as easily succumb to the programmatic, as in the case of Myles's crass repudiation of Lowell. In this case, the "format" conforms to the personal brand rather than the tradition.

It might be argued that I have gravitated with this example to the lowest uncommon denominator, though Eileen Myles's work has assumed considerable branding over the last few years and is not at a loss for critical attention and ample consideration for awards. Branding can be power, of a certain kind, and that includes the power to demean, condemn, and trivialize. Perhaps "The Death of Robert Lowell" might best be called an "anti-identity" poem fueled by an anti-poetic animus—to unmake rather than make, to place another's unmaking at the forefront of one's own writerly ambitions. It does not seem to be the most constructive motivation or the most exemplary of accomplishments. In any case, Myles's poem is also about branding, in this case the branding of Robert Lowell—old coot, loon, wasp, famous poet of undeniable social and historical privilege—for post-mortem trivialization, execution, erasure: fucking dead. The poet who wrote "The Quaker Graveyard in Nantucket" and more than a few other poems worthy of the utmost admiration, deserves better, regardless of how one might feel personally about his privilege, family history, social status, and personal failures.

The problem with what goes by the shorthand "identity poetry" is that those who employ the phrase, whether critically or descriptively, often lose sight of the fact that subject matter does not become content until it has been brought under the shaping jurisdiction of form. Such shaping jurisdiction can be realized "formally openly or brokenly" and does not involve any "mechanical fidelity to inherited rules."[227] From this perspective, Myles's "The Death of Robert Lowell" lacks more than good taste; it lacks the artistic realization even of its passionate political urgency. When I encounter this kind of flippant contempt for genuine artistry in the face of some personal or social animus, I find myself resisting the phrase "identity poetry." From one perspective, it appears to empower—I have heard students and other poets use the phrase or some variation appreciatively—while from another it instantiates anew the very marginalization it claims to redress.

In masterful hands, however, a poem achieves the kind of intendedness and complexity that places the reader or listener genuinely in the nexus of intractable emotions, ideas, cultural and personal inheritances. Such is Natasha Trethewey's "Pastoral":

> In the dream, I am with the Fugitive
> Poets. We're gathered for a photograph.
> Behind us, the skyline of Atlanta
> hidden by the photographer's backdrop—
> a lush pasture, green, full of soft-eyed cows
> lowing, a chant that sounds like *no, no. Yes*
> I say to the glass of bourbon I'm offered.
> We're lining up now—Robert Penn Warren,
> his voice just audible above the drone
> of bulldozers, telling us where to stand.
> Say "*race*," the photographer croons. I'm in
> blackface again when the flash freezes us.
> *My father's white*, I tell them, and *rural*.
> *You don't hate the south? They ask. You don't hate it?*[228]

Trethewey's blank sonnet, her use of the form as much a nod to Robert Lowell as to the Fugitives, at once evokes and interrogates, and refuses to stoop to vitriolic condemnation and lampoon. The ironic "pastoral" of her title at once conjures the complexity and injustices of that tradition—European and the American south—and contests that tradition. If Yeats is right in saying that out of the quarrel with others one makes rhetoric and out of the quarrel with self, poetry, then Eileen Myles's "The Death of Robert Lowell" is nothing more than an empty rhetorical contrivance. By contrast, Trethewey's "Pastoral" is a brilliantly achieved manifestation of the argument with self that has broad positive repercussions aesthetically, socially, and politically. The wonderful sleight of that "no, no, Yes" embodies all of the dynamics of the poem's raw contraries. Just outside the poem, the bulldozers are paving the Fugitives's traditionalist paradise. Inside the poem, as it moves to its end, and with the most erudite and incisive irony, all of the most vexing and painful aspects of the American experience and American poetry gain purchase and are given not an answer but the clarity of artistic form—the specter of hatred raised, confronted, and left un-indulged.

Trethewey's "Pastoral" ends unsettlingly, intentionally so, and leaves its reader in an unsettled state. Good poems and certainly great poems always do just that. They leave us there in the experience of a quandary—the quandary of the poet's being that has transcended itself into the poem. The specific quandary, the specific quarrel with self, may not be our own, but we come to share its life in the life of the poem through the transformation of mere subject matter into genuine content. To brand something, conversely, is to seek to settle the matter, is to stipulate an orientation that ultimately precludes art's fullest amplitude. That is because great art refuses labels, brands, even the label "Emily Dickinson," just by way of example. One must go to the poems, one aftermath of the poet's life, and become unsettled. That is why in our own milieu there is something restrictive and potentially condescending (depending on the source offering the label) about the branding of poets. The Fugitives identified themselves as much to define what they intended artistically and ethically, but even such self-branding must eventually give way to the poem performed and received in the mind of the reader, the listener. Poetry at its most achieved eludes the brand, even in this late overly commodified moment when poets feel the pressure to be media marketers of their work. The best poems remind us that to be human, to be on serious earth, is to be unequivocally unsettled. They remind us that no univocal label can finally accommodate the fullness and richness of human experience. What is needed, contrarily, is the insight of identity discovered in and through difference—that is the analogical necessity. In an essay, happily titled "The Transcendent Poem," Laura Kasischke quotes Laura (Riding) Jackson on Jackson's renunciation of poetry. "Corruption of the reason for poetry sets in," Jackson writes, "when too much emphasis is laid on assisting the reader, when the reader goes to poetry with no notion whatever of the faculties required, the poet is more concerned with stirring up the required faculties than presenting occasions for exercising them."[229] Whatever comes to be popular in poetry for a time must inevitably find life beyond the brand or settle into some manner of corruption, so Jackson's reflections imply.

And where is our third figure now at the hoopla of commencement, the poet heretic in the baseball cap among the sea of rippling gowns, chevrons loosening, the hood draped behind like an un-spread plumage? Our poet heretic moves, e pluribus unum, among the crowd filing out of the arena, in hand a book of poems.

EPILOGUE: WHAT IS THE QUESTION?

In the photograph, the old poet looks out from the half-door of his stone cottage as from the inside of a prehistoric cave, but for the swung-open window sash abutting a leafless shrub. He's leaning out, more than a little grimly it seems, his left hand resting on the lower jamb, in his right a pair of reading glasses held firmly. The poet's face is a sharp-edged crag, his mouth turned slightly down, the hair around his bald pate a simmering white flame waiting to increase wildly with the first breeze. The eyes looking a little away at something off-center glare fiercely. So appeared R.S. Thomas, called by then "The Ogre of Wales," near the end of his life. Born in 1913 two years after Charles Olson, who coined the word "postmodern" in a letter to Robert Creeley, and a year before John Berryman, whose psychically fraught poems anticipate and enact the postmodern predicament of metaphysical vacuity and the poet's need to respond with self-performance and linguistic play, Thomas confronted all of the same epistemological, ontological and aesthetic insecurities of the 20th century on into the 21st. He died in the year 2000 at the age of eighty-seven. His first two books were self-published, the second by a printer with a one-room office above a chipper, though the books that followed brought him progressively greater renown until, four years before his death, he was nominated for the Nobel Prize. A priest for nearly forty years in the Church of Wales, a prolific and prodigious poet whose work many believe to be among greatest to have been produced in English in the 20th century, Thomas is still barely acknowledged in the expansive but simultaneously closed circles of American poetry. Extraordinarily, he managed to shape his ever more intellectually, emotionally, and spiritually urgent body of work by making his artistic journey against the grain of a progressively more secular and technologically driven world. He also, quite literally, moved farther out and deeper into the far reaches of Wales— to Aberdaron on the remote Llyn peninsula where he held his last rectorship, and finally to the cottage at Sarn-y-Pla on the same remote peninsula near a place called Porth Neigul, Hell's Mouth. If Stephanie Burt's gloss that "the poets with the fewest hip connections, farthest from the metropolitan centers, are the likeliest to get overlooked"[230] carries enduring relevance, then Thomas's career is surely among the more remarkable in recent memory being so steadfastly un-branded. In a rather stunning synchronicity, he lost the Nobel in literature to Seamus Heaney in 1996, another great poet born to unlikely circumstances who rose by temperament and his particular genius into the pivotal center of literary fame and world regard.

R.S. Thomas, by contrast, was by temperament and artistic inclination a contrarian, an outlier. One thinks of Dickinson, Hopkins, and Bishop his relative contemporary, rather than Pound or Lowell, and certainly not Stein, who cultivated her legend with extreme prejudice—Thomas was a middle-class Welshman who spoke with a cultivated English accent, who taught himself Welsh later in life but would write his poems in English; a priest who felt more at home wandering the hills bird watching than among his parishioners. Though he fulfilled his ministerial duties with care, especially visiting the sick, and performed his sacramental duties with dedication, all the while he rigorously questioned his faith and its most basic principles. He was a pacifist who refused to condemn Welsh nationalists who fire-bombed English vacation homes; a father who packed his son, Gwydion, off to English boarding school to give more time to himself and his wife, the painter Mildred "Elsi" Eldridge, to write and paint. Principally, he was a poet whose work faces head-on the limits of language, the onslaught of materialist philosophy, and the advance of science as the dominant prism by which human beings take stock of reality. He also faces with ferocious courage the lurking emptiness behind the self's apparent solvency, its consciousness, its sense of presence. His work in short takes on the lineaments of the nominalist universe that comes to full fruition in the postmodern milieu, but does so in a way that eschews the indulgences of postmodernist aesthetics.

In postmodernism, language is assumed to be a closed system. Consequently, postmodernist poetry feels quite at home in the endless play of the language game. The idea of a rupture between language and reality is not unfamiliar to Thomas's poetry. As he reflects in "Epitaph, "The poem in the rock / and the poem in the mind / are not one."[231] More troubling, in "The Gap" Thomas posits the scenario of God awakening "but the nightmare did not recede." Instead, "word by word / the tower of speech grew" to the point where, as with the tower of Babel to which the poem alludes[232] "vocabulary would have triumphed" where God rests "on the chasm a / word could bridge." Except in Thomas's riff of the story of Babel, God leaves "the blank / still by his name of the same / order as the territory / between them / the verbal hunger for the thing itself." The blank of God's true name nullifies the bridge any word might make to the thing itself and so to reality. R.S. Thomas and Charles Bernstein would appear to be, incongruously, on the same page—there is no way beyond language to bridge to reality. What follows in the poem marks the difference between Thomas's postmodern vision and language poetry's doctrinal postmodernism:

> And the darkness
> that is a god's blood swelled
> in him, and he let it
> to make the sign in the space
> on the page, that is all languages
> and none; that is the grammarian's
> torment and the mystery
> at the cell's core, and the equation
> that will not come out, and is
> the narrowness that we stare
> over into the eternal
> silence that is the repose of God.[233]

For Thomas, the gap that inevitably presents itself in language—that space resident in the sign like a mote in the eye—is the signal of the mystery resident "at the cell's core" and also in the unsolvable equation of physical being. It signals the infinite depth of things rather than the shallows. Rather than the word, this apophatic blank is the sign of God, the sign that points to the via negativa the poet must traverse. As he declares in "Waiting":

> Face to face? Ah, no
> God; such language falsifies
> the relation. Nor side by side,
> nor near you, nor anywhere
> in time and space.[234]

Does Thomas as priest and poet believe that in the beginning there was the Blank and not the Word, that only a negating emptiness underlies the Logos? In one sense, it seems so. In another, it does not. For "a word" is not "The Word" in Thomas's conception of life and poetry. The relation that links them is founded on God's side of the gap or not at all. That relation, as we have seen, is analogical, mediatory, a leap as between synapses across the empty gap permitted, of all things, by God's own self-emptying. That leap, that bridge, Simone Weil would have recognized as made possible by God. In Weil's theology, creation is only made possible by God's withdrawal, like an infinite ocean receding to reveal a shore. We find the same concept in the Kabbalah, and God's tzimtzum, God's contraction into the Ein Sof, the fiat that permits creation to be at all. In a similar fashion, Thomas's God cannot be an object, an agent alongside other agents, however greater.[235] It is the Absence that allows for the very presence of the world, as well as the world's longing for what is more than world. "It is this great absence / that is like a presence that compels / me to address it without hope / of a reply," Thomas states outright in "The Absence," and he continues: "My equations fail / as my words do. What resource have I / other than the emptiness without him of my whole / being, a vacuum he may not abhor?"[236] Such is Thomas's version of the deus absconditus, the absent or hidden God. This God has deep roots in western contemplative and theological traditions, and Thomas's poetry, like Simone Weil's philosophy of divine withdrawal, makes those traditions relevant for our own time.

It is this "absent" God's "eternal silence" that requires a renovated understanding of Eternity. As Thomas urged in an interview in *Poetry Wales*:

> I firmly believe this, that eternity is not something out there, not something in the future; it is close to us, it is all around us and at any given moment we can pass into it; but there is something about our mortality, the fact that we are time-bound creatures, that makes it somehow difficult if not impossible to dwell . . . to dwell permanently in that . . . .[237]

By comparison, Gertrude Stein's "continuous present" is a faux eternity, a turning aside from the time-bound nature of writing in which its native action must take place. All the more so Paul Hoover's facile "Ethernity." That momentary apprehension of eternity emergent or irruptive for the moment in time is, as Paul Ricoeur might say, the ultimate Surplus, a divine abundance, the basis for all surpluses of meaning. In a statement that would catch any remotely orthodox person off-guard, Thomas once said "resurrection is metaphor." Metaphor: the very stuff of language signaling across the gap, the dynamic holding together of sameness and difference connecting eternity and time, God and world. Metaphor. Metaxu. The bridge by which an empty sign comes to signify the meaningful word, the analogical relation by which the world is seen as world. Thomas evokes this shaping insight in "The Answer":

> There have been times
> when, after long on my knees
> in a cold chancel, a stone has rolled
> from my mind, and I have looked
> in and seen the old questions lie
> folded in a place
> by themselves, like the piled
> graveclothes of love's risen body.[238]

Or as he says with even more visionary urgency in his poem "Alive":

> Looking out I can see
> no death . . . the darkness
> is the deepening shadow
> or your presence: the silence a
> process in the metabolism
> of the being a love.[239]

The final lines of "Alive" demonstrate how Thomas assimilates diction and metaphor from modern science as well as from religious practice, especially mystical theology. This amalgamation of different kinds of language—the scientific and the religious—accords with the range of diction found in many postmodern poems. The difference is that in Thomas's work such amalgamations suggest and presume an underlying cohesiveness, an analogical relation. Still, the alignment between Thomas's poetry and postmodernism remains ironic since Thomas himself was so adamantly at odds with the modern world—his wife Elsi removed the heating fixtures from their Sarn cottage, this in their old age. When still a rector Thomas preached against the use of refrigerators! No wonder in "Emerging" Thomas finds himself awaiting God on "some peninsula of the spirit." The poet turns his back on traditionally religious "anthropomorphisms of the fancy" that encouraged the generations to watch in vain for the Hand to descend out of the clouds. Instead, he envisions the advent of a God revealed from below rather than from above:

> We are beginning to see
> now it is matter is the scaffolding
> of the spirit: that the poem emerges
> from morphemes and phonemes
> [...]
> so in everyday life
> it is the plain facts and natural happenings
> that conceal God and reveal him to us
> little by little under the mind's tooling.[240]

In Thomas's understanding of things, it is the reductive stuff of material life and language that compound to form the "scaffolding" of a meaningfulness that transcends our ability to fully represent it. "Emerging" combines a vision of material reality very close to that of Teilhard de Chardin—the universe as divine milieu. Thomas's poem also resonates with Ricoeur's conception of language as surpluses of meanings ranging across scales from semiological to syntactical to metaphorical. It is at the scale of metaphor, again, that language's true nature reveals itself as part of an analogical reality—emergent rather than handed down "from above." Yet, it is precisely at the "higher" scale of metaphor that language's ultimate nature resides. To claim the "true" nature of language resides in signs is to miss the proverbial forest for the trees, the living, breathing body for the parts that compose it. In view of Augustine's idea of the sentence as the form whose meaning requires the existence of time and memory, reductionism fixes meaning to the atomistic space of discrete signs—the nominal—and thereby denies real temporal movement. It petrifies the essential drama of the real. Meaning is in this dramatic movement, not in the static "continuous present" of signifiers forever misfiring to no end.

We find material reality and language "emergent" again in Thomas's late poem, "The Promise," where he writes:

> From nothing
> nothing comes. Behind everything—
> something, somebody? In the beginning
> violence, the floor of the universe
> littered with fragments. After
> that enormous brawl, where
> did the dove come from?[241]

Thomas's run of questions penetrating back to beginnings demonstrates that, for this poet, the quest for ultimate meaning takes place in and *as* a contested arena of consciousness. Thomas's poetry is filled with as much spiritual angst and bitterness, in fact, as epiphanies—a good deal more angst and bitterness, as in the poem "A Species":

> Shipwrecked upon an island
> in a universe whose tides
> are the winds, they began multiplying
> without joy. They cut down the trees
> to have room to make money.[242]

So much for Donne's "No man is an island." The species is shipwrecked here, consuming the singular place that might sustain it while the planet keeps "blue with cold, waiting to be loved." The astounding human capacity for destruction, for self-destruction, originates for Thomas in a misalliance between the species's material existence and the love that would emerge, but does so only occasionally. As Thomas remarks in "Incubation," "In the absence of such wings / as were denied us we insist / on inheriting others from the machine."[243] The machine is Thomas's word for what we have brought ourselves to and for what at times seems an almost Manichean negation: we appear to be "denied" wings. Such is his judgment.

This brings us to the nature of subjectivity in Thomas's poetry, which—unlike the disembodied, postmodernist self—refuses to relinquish identity to a performance of absence, a performance that often comes off more as egotistical pose than compelling encounter. Nor do Thomas's poems build a fortress around some unassailable "I." The landscape of self is very nearly always dramatically contested:

> A man's shadow
> falls upon rocks that are
> millions of years old, and
> thought comes to drink at that dark
> pool, but goes away thirsty.[244]

In "Senior," a potentially narcissistic scene reveals the thirst of consciousness for something that might transcend it. The mind's thirst is insatiable, and profoundly sad, but it is also the trace of divine longing, the longing that is itself divine by being withdrawn—at once in and of the dark. That does not make the mind, like the poem, any less a contested space. "Is there a place / here for the spirit," Thomas asks in "Balance," "is there time / on this brief platform for anything / other than mind's failure to explain itself?"[245] Or again, more personally, as he confesses in "Inside":

> I am my own
> geology, strata on strata
> of the imagination, tufa
> dreams, the limestone mind
> honeycombed by the running away
> of too much thought.[246]

Here, the poet's mind assumes a kind of a sublime vastness out of Wordsworth's "The Prelude," but quickly reveals itself to be a cavernous realm where thoughts and ideas like stalactites and stalagmites solidify into rigidity. They "reify," to use a word common in the postmodernist lexicon, to where truth at bottom is only a "cold, locationless" cloud. For all of Thomas's religious feeling and imagination there is no turning away from the specter of the mind harkening back to the human beginning—a materialist maze. Thomas's psychic universe, his imaginative universe, remains a contested territory where postmodernism's summary negations are confronted with depth and urgency rather than endless parody. Eternity may be nearby, like the bright field in Thomas's poem of that title, "the pearl of great price," but for the poet God is a raptor hunting us down, and all of us "lesser denizens" of an intractable universe.[247] The sum of the poet's conflicted thoughts place him on a threshold—a postmodern threshold, yes, but also a threshold native to the human enigma regardless of time, culture, or circumstance. Where we are, here, is nothing like a continuous present. Instead, we find ourselves on a vantage ground surveying, bridging the connections, the disconnections, the order, and the chaos. As "Threshold" counsels, the liminal space, the crux of time on which we always stand, requires present and continuous *action*:

> I emerge from the mind's
> cave into the worse darkness
> outside, where things pass and
> the Lord is in none of them.
>
> I have heard the still, small voice
> and it is that of the bacteria
> demolishing my cosmos. I
> have lingered too long on
>
> this threshold, but where can I go?
> To look back is to lose the soul
> I was leading upward towards
> the light. To look forward? Ah,
>
> what balance is needed at
> the edge of such an abyss.
> I am alone on the surface

Of a turning planet. What

to do but, like Michelangelo's
Adam, put my hand
out into unknown space,
hoping for the reciprocating touch?[248]

Thomas's "Threshold" reverses the expectations inherent in the old story of the residents of Plato's cave rising to the light and transforms it into a spiritual nightmare. It also, startlingly, dislodges our habitual take on Michelangelo's magnificent image of Adam reaching his hand toward God's on the Sistine Chapel ceiling by essentially erasing the anthropomorphized Deity from the scene. We are on the very edge of absence, blankness, erasure—the postmodern condition of anti-metaphysics. There are no fire-fangled feathers dangling down. Thomas's poetry brings us to this space, this black hole, only with the true existential urgency that resides behind the condition which has always been at the *spiritual* threshold of the species.

And "Threshold" leaves us in the erasure, or rather in an agon of waiting before the ultimate absence, which may be the absence of the ultimate. It brings us to the limit of the analogical understanding of being—brings us to the paradoxical reality of the Nothing-That-Is, to paraphrase Wallace Stevens's "The Snow Man," or a window to the brink that shows nothing and is nowhere and is endless, to echo Larkin. Or is it, as for Meister Eckhart, the apophatic threshold where we begin to sense the "Godhead beyond God.? In "The Other," on the other hand, listening to an owl calling at night, and the swells rising and falling on the Atlantic "on the long shore / by the village, that is without light / and companionless," Thomas with supreme negative capability watches the thought come to him "of that other being who is awake, too, / letting our prayers break on him, / not like this for a few hours, / but for days, years, for eternity."[249] In "The Other," Thomas imagines if only momentarily the reciprocating gesture he waits for in "Threshold." Though, again, the gesture does not match expectations, perhaps now because the poet has relinquished all expectations and merely lets the sound of waves, the being of things, break on him. In "The Other," the vision of God as some omnipotent immoveable mover, some presiding "transcendental signifier" that guarantees all we might say about ourselves, falls away. What we are left with is a vision of God as Other, Octavio Paz's primordial Other—a Love so encompassing it levels the distance between the material and immaterial, between immanence and transcendence, absence and presence, time and eternity. It does so by virtue of the gap between all binaries, and it does so without collapsing that gap, for the gap *is* the necessary threshold that brings us to Thomas's encounter with ultimacy. Established in the gap separating that infinite Other from finite mind is the connection—at once asynchronous and synchronous—that embodies the analogical relation as the pure renunciation of divine power in favor of divine compassion. Here the unavoidable human penchant for conceiving God in anthropomorphic terms—even as pure spiritual consciousness—distills into reciprocating relation, I–Thou: the other recognizing the true depth of longing and love in the Other.

For all of R.S. Thomas's resistance to modernity, his poetry confronts the most enduring epistemological and ontological concerns that inform and underlie the crisis of postmodernism, and that have haunted us as a species from our beginnings. For many poets, ultimate questions of meaning and aesthetic value no longer rise to the surface of critical concern. The exhaustion of meaning and value is simply the nature of things. We merely have been deluding ourselves for centuries. We no longer have need of these, or any supreme fictions. Perhaps not surprisingly, of all modern poets Thomas most valued Wallace Stevens, for his artistry but also for his ideas on poetry and religion. The final lines of Thomas's "Homage to Wallace Stevens" address the poet with whom he felt the greatest kinship:

> Blessings Stevens;
> I stand with my back to grammar
> at an altar you never aspired
> to celebrating the sacrament
> of the imagination whose high-priest
> notwithstanding you are.[250]

Echoes of Stevens's "The Idea of Order at Key West" and "The Palm at the End of the Mind" haunt Thomas's poems "The Other" and "Threshold." All place the reader on the edge of vastness, sublime in Stevens's case, though more temperamentally transcendent in the case of Thomas. Both poets through their individual prisms view the imagination as sacred and poetry as an inherently religious art. It is remarkable that two poets of the most disparate sensibilities, R.S. Thomas and John Ashbery, trace equally their aesthetic ancestry to Wallace Stevens, such that one could further chart the polarities of the postmodern world by way of these two guiding stars. What we find here again is the heretic's choice of orthodoxies. Or as Thomas reflects in "Heretics," his poem that considers the power of human congregations:

> Are they selective
> like me, knowing that among
> a myriad disciplines each one
> has its orthodoxy from which
> the words flow? Alas, we are heretics all . . . . [251]

And yet, in view of our circumstance, the Welsh poet chooses the heresy of finding meaning in the world beyond the play of surfaces and with hope for "the kingdom" that would render all our heretical foolishness worthwhile, and without which all worth fritters away into poses, displays, empty gestures, congregations of power and will.

Near the end of his life, in an encounter made for documentary footage, R.S. Thomas met Czeslaw Milosz for dinner. In the Irish poet Dennis O'Driscoll's account, it was an extraordinary night with two of the great religious poets of the 20th century exchanging their experiences, a meeting of two imposingly creative minds. At evening's end, the two parted from each other agreeing: *We are both on the way to extinction.*[252] Reflecting on what he calls our "post-human" world, theologian David Bentley Hart calls to mind that "innumerable forces are vying for the future, and Christianity may prove considerably weaker than its rivals."[253] No cause for despair, since faith is not merely "a cultural logic" but must be believed to be "a cosmic truth, which can never finally be defeated."[254] The answer, Hart ventures, is to embrace being an outlier, like the desert faithful at the start of the Christian empire—a kind of protest against worldly power, cultural power, however delusively well-intentioned. Though to do so surely would mean living "in a painful state of tension."[255] Though Thomas and Milosz saw themselves on the way to extinction, both would have assented to trusting in a critical assumption of truth underlying the materials, to trusting in our limited human abilities to represent that truth and the world that truth sustains.

At a time when contemporary poetry seems to have all the channel choice of cable television or direct TV or, more accurately, self-programmed iPads, iPods, and iPhones, the assent to any idea of truth—truth that would dispose us toward the other—appears remote. What is at stake, as Nicholas Carr reminds us in his disturbing *The Shallows*, is the progressive erosion of our ability to read and think deeply, which is exactly what our pervasive reliance on the internet appears to have accomplished—an unforeseen result of its power and convenience. Brain plasticity, that sine-qua-non of our species, primes us for adaptation. The problem is that our neurons and synapses are "entirely indifferent . . . to the quality of our thought," which means the skills we gain in surfing the Net, often distractedly along the shallows of information coming at us, may well be far less valuable than the skills we lose.[256] What we are losing, progressively, is "the literary brain," the brain that requires the "meditative act," that allows for "the unique mental process of deep reading."[257] By disengaging ourselves from "the outward flow of passing stimuli in order to engage more deeply with the inward flow of words, ideas, and emotions," our attention ceases to engage with or experience the liberating act of contemplation.[258] The kind of contemplative mind Carr desires to preserve? He finds it in Wallace Stevens's "The House was Quiet and the World was Calm":

> The reader became the book; and summer night
>
> was like the conscious being of the book.
> [. . .]
>
> The quiet was part of the meaning, part of the mind:
> The access of perfection to the page. [259]

The Web, alas, is built for speed, constant input, the shallow connectivity of rapid links and jumps, so as companies "like Google and Microsoft perfect search engines for video and audio content, more products are undergoing the fragmentation that already characterizes written works."[260] Such concerns have already been embedded in Paul Hoover's utopian embrace of postmodernist fragmentation, his celebration of poetry's shallows, the flatland of poetry as wallpaper. Though approaching the problem from alternate perspectives, the one theological, the other sociological and scientific, David Bentley Hart and Nicholas Carr come to essentially the same conclusion: where we are heading constitutes "a reversal of the trajectory of civilization" as well as a "slow erosion of our humanness and our humanity."[261] Poetry, that art form so deeply bound to the origins of human culture and civilization, should be positioned prophetically against this leveling trend.

"Why is the human brain the most complex object known to exist in the universe?' Marilynne Robinson asks in *Absence of Mind*. One answer, resonant with the view that human consciousness is a chemical mistake, is "because the elaborations of the mammalian brain that promoted the survival of the organism have overshot the mark." Her other ardently preferred answer? "Because it is intrinsic to our role in the universe as thinkers and perceivers, participants in a singular capacity for wonder as well as comprehension."[262] Dying of stomach cancer at the end of her life, her life's work a triumph of the shallows, Gertrude Stein spoke her last words: "What is the answer?" When Alice B. Toklas could not give her an answer, Stein asked in turn: "In that case, what is the question?"[263] It is common for a writer, like anyone, not to have *the* answer, but it is sad to have written and lived in a manner never to have known the question, or to have inhabited that question, that ultimate question, in one's life and art. Here, implicit in Marilynne Robinson's Kierkegaardian "either/or" is the question, posed as it always is against the shadow of death: "And what then?" R.S. Thomas's answer, given after the death of his beloved wife, in the poem "No Time," is unequivocal:

> I look up in recognition
> of a presence in absence.

Not a word, not a sound,
as she goes her way,
but a scent lingering
which is that of time immolating
itself in love's fire.[264]

Thomas's answer, even at this late time, is worthy of many another poet who would sustain tradition even as the tradition renovates and evolves; it is the answer to a question that, if left unasked, unacknowledged, or unknown, will continue to impoverish the poet and the poet's art.

BIBLIOGRAPHY

Abrams, David. *The Spell of the Sensuous: Perception and Language in a More-Than-Human World.* New York: Vintage, 1996.

Ammons, A.R. *Set in Motion.* Ann Arbor, MI: University of Michigan Press, 1996.

Ashbery, John. *Selected Poems.* New York: Farrar, Straus and Giroux, 1985.

Auden, W.H. *The Dyer's Hand.* New York: Random House, 1990.

Augustine of Hippo. *Confessions.* New York: Penguin, 1961.

Barbarasi, Albert-Laszlo. "The Physics of the Web," *Physics World* (July, 2001).

Barfield, Owen. *Poetic Diction, Poetic Form: A Study in Meaning.* Hanover, NH: University Press of New England, 1973.

Barfield, Owen. *The Rediscovery of Meaning.* Oxford: Barfield Press, 2013.

Barfield, Owen. *Saving the Appearances: A Study in Idolatry.* New York: Harcourt, Brace, Jovanovich, 1946.

Barth, John. *Further Fridays.* Boston: Back Bay Books, 1996.

Benfey, Christopher. "The Alibi of Ambiguity," *The New Republic* (June 28, 2012).

Bernstein, Charles. *Content's Dream.* Chicago: Northwestern University Press, 1986.

Bernstein, Charles. *Girly Man.* Chicago: University of Chicago Press, 2006.

Bernstein, Charles. *Recalculating.* Chicago: University of Chicago Press, 2013.

Bernstein, Charles. "Time Out of Motion: Looking Ahead to See Backwards." In *Conversant Essays.* Detroit: Wayne State University Press, 1990.

Burt, Stephanie [originally published under the name Stephen Burt]. *Close Calls with Nonsense.* St. Paul: Graywolf, 2009.

Carr, Nicholas. *The Shallows: What the Internet is Doing to Our Brains.* New York: W.W. Norton, 2011.

Carson, Anne. *Decreation.* New York: Alfred Knopf, 2005.

Casson, Christine. "Historical Narrative in the Lyric Sequence." In *The*

Contemporary Narrative Poem. Ed. Stephen P. Schneider. Iowa City: University of Iowa Press, 2013.

Collins, Billy. *Aimless Love: New and Selected Poems.* New York: Random House, 2014.

Collins, Billy. *Picnic, Lightning.* Pittsburgh: University of Pittsburgh Press, 1998.

Collins, Billy. *Questions About Angels.* Pittsburgh: University of Pittsburgh Press, 2003.

Dickinson, Emily. Complete Poems. Ed. Thomas Johnson. New York: Little Brown, 1960.

Dickman, Michael. *Flies.* Port Townsend, WA: Copper Canyon Press, 2011.

Dodds, E.R. *Pagan and Christian in an Age of Anxiety.* New York: W.W. Norton, 1965.

Dupré, Louis. *Transcendent Selfhood: The Loss and Rediscovery of the Inner Self.* New York: Seabury Press, 1976.

Dyson, Freeman. *Infinite in All Directions.* New York: Perennial, 2004.

Eliot, T.S. *The Use of Poetry and the Use of Criticism.* London: Faber and Faber, 1933.

Eliot, T.S. *Selected Prose of T.S. Eliot.* Ed. Frank Kermode. New York: Harcourt, Brace, Jovanovich, 1975.

Fairchild, B.H. *The Art of the Lathe.* Farmington, ME: Alice James Books, 1998.

Fields, Stephen M. *Analogies of Transcendence: An Essay on Nature, Grace, and Modernity.* Washington, DC: Catholic University of America Press, 2016.

Glück, Louise. *The Wild Iris.* New York: Ecco, 1993.

Harari, Yuval Noah. *Sapiens: A Brief History of Humankind.* New York: Harper Collins, 2015.

Hart, David Bentley. *Atheist Delusions.* New Haven: Yale University Press, 2009.

Hart, David Bentley. *The Experience of God.* New Haven, CT: Yale University Press, 2013.

Hart, David Bentley. *The Beauty of the Infinite.* Grand Rapids, MI: Eerdmans, 2003.

Hayden, Robert. *Collected Poems*. Ed. Frederick Glaysher. New York: Liveright, 1985.

Hayden, Robert. *Collected Prose*. Ed. Frederick Glaysher. Ann Arbor, MI: University of Michigan Press, 1984.

Hoagland, Tony. *Real Sofistikayshun*. St. Paul, MN: Graywolf, 2006.

Hobhouse, Janet. *Everybody Who Was Anybody: A Biography of Gertrude Stein*. New York: G.P. Putnam's Sons, 1975.

Hoover, Paul. *Postmodern American Poetry II*. New York: W.W. Norton, 2009.

Hoover, Paul. *Postmodern American Poetry*. First Edition. New York: W.W. Norton, 2001.

Hudgins, Andrew. *Ecstatic in the Poison*. New York: Overlook, 2003.

Hungerford, Amy. *Postmodern Belief: American Literature and Religion Since 1960*. Princeton, NJ: Princeton University Press, 2010.

Jarrell, Randall. *Poetry and the Age*. Gainesville, FL: University Press of Florida, 2001.

Kermode, Frank. *The Sense of an Ending*. London: Oxford University Press, 2000.

Komunyakaa, Yusef. *Neon Vernacular: New and Selected Poems*. Middleton, CT: Wesleyan University Press, 1993.

Larkin, Philip. *The Collected Poems*. New York: Farrar, Straus and Giroux, 2004.

Levinas, Emanuel. *Time and the Other*. Pittsburgh: Duquesne University Press, 1990.

Lynch, William. *Christ and Apollo: Dimensions of the Literary Imagination*. New York: Intercollegiate Studies, 2003.

Milosz, Czeslaw. *The Witness of Poetry*. Cambridge, MA: Harvard University Press, 1984.

Nelson, Marilyn. "Owning the Masters." In *After New Formalism*. Ed. Annie Finch. Brownsville, OR: Story Line Press, 1999.

O'Driscoll, Dennis. *The Outnumbered Poet*. Loughcrew, Ireland: Gallery Press, 2012.

O'Driscoll, Dennis. *Stepping Stones: Interviews with Seamus Heaney*. New York: Farrar, Straus and Giroux, 2008.

Oliver, Mary. *Devotions: The Selected Poems of Mary Oliver*. New York: Penguin, 2017.

Oliver, Mary. *New and Selected Poems: Volume One*. Boston: Beacon Press, 1992.

Olson, Charles. *Projective Verse*. New York: Totem Press, 1959.

Pagels, Elaine. *The Gnostic Gospels*. New York: Vintage, 1979.

Paz, Octavio. *The Bow and the Lyre*. Austin: University of Texas Press, 2009.

Pelikan, Jarislav. *The Emergence of the Catholic Tradition (100–600)*. Chicago: University of Chicago Press, 1971.

Perloff, Marjorie, *The Poetics of Indeterminacy*. Princeton, NJ: Princeton University Press, 1981.

Phillips, Carl. *Coin of the Realm*. St. Paul, MN: Graywolf, 2007.

Phillips, D.Z. *R.S. Thomas: Poet of the Hidden God*. London: Wipf and Stock, 1986.

Pinsky, Robert. *Poetry and the World*. New York: Ecco Press, 1980.

Pinsky, Robert. *The Situation of Poetry*. Princeton, NJ: Princeton University Press, 1978.

Rich, Adrienne. "Format and Form," in After the New Formalism. Ed. Annie Finch (Ashland, OR: Story Line Press, 1999), 6.

Ricoeur, Paul. *The Philosophy of Paul Ricoeur*. Eds. Charles E. Regan and David Stewart. Boston: Beacon Press, 1978.

Robinson, Marilynne. *Absence of Mind*. New Haven, CT: Yale University Press, 2010.

Scarry, Elaine. *The Body in Pain: The Making and Unmaking of the World*. London: Oxford University Press, 1987.

Silliman, Ron. "Postmodernism: Sign for a Struggle, Struggle for a Sign." In *Conversant Essays: Contemporary Poets on Poetry*. Ed. James McCorkle. Detroit: Wayne State University Press, 1990.

Sleigh, Thomas. *Interview With a Ghost*. Minneapolis: Graywolf Press, 2006.

Smith, Derik. *Robert Hayden in Verse*. Ann Arbor, MI: University of Michigan Press, 2018.

Stein, Gertrude. *Wars I Have Seen*. London: BT Batsford, 1945.

Stein, Gertrude. "Composition as Explanation." In *Gertrude Stein: Writings and Lectures 1909–1945*. Ed. Patricia Meyerowitz. New York: Penguin Books, 1967.

Stevens, Wallace. *The Collected Poems of Wallace Stevens*. New York: Vintage, 1990.

Stevens, Wallace. *The Necessary Angel*. New York: Vintage, 1951.

Stevens, Wallace. *The Palm at the End of the Mind*. New York: Vintage, 1990.

Strand, Mark. *Collected Poems*. New York: Knopf, 2014.

Thomas, R.S. *Collected Poems, 1945–1990*. London: Phoenix, 1993.

Thomas, R.S. *No Truce with the Furies*. Northumberland, UK: Bloodaxe, 1995.

Thomas, R.S. *The Poems of R.S. Thomas*. Scottsdale, AZ: University if Arizona Press, 1985.

Tobin, Daniel and Pimone Triplett, Eds. *Poet's Work, Poet's Play*. Ann Arbor, MI: University of Michigan Press, 2007.

Tracy, David. *The Analogical Imagination*. New York: Crossroads, 1986.

Weil, Simone. *A Simone Weil Reader*. New York: Moyer Bell, 2007.

Weil, Simone. *Waiting for God*. New York: Harper Collins Perennial Classics, 2009.

Weil, Simone. *Gravity and Grace*. London: Routledge, 1952.

Weil, Simone. *The Need for Roots*. London: Routledge and Kegan, 1987.

Williams, C.K. *Poetry and Consciousness*. Ann Arbor, MI: University of Michigan Press, 1998.

Yeats, William Butler. *The Collected Poems of W. B. Yeats*. New York: Scribner, 1996.

Yeats, W.B. *Essays and Introductions*. New York: Collier Books, 1961.

NOTES

[1] *Plato: The Collected Dialogues*. Eds. Edith Hamilton and Huntington Cairns. (Princeton, NJ: Princeton University Press, 1961).

[2] Simone Weil, *Gravity and Grace* (London: Routledge, 2002), 146.

[3] Philip Larkin, *Collected Poems* (New York: Farrar, Straus and Giroux, 2004), 58.

[4] Octavio Paz, *The Bow and the Lyre* (Austin, TX: University of Texas Press, 2009), 131.

[5] Ibid., 246–7.

[6] Ibid., 168–9.

[7] Ibid., 262.

[8] Simone Weil, *Simone Weil Reader* (New York: Moyer Bell, 2007), 363.

[9] Dennis O'Driscoll, *Stepping Stones* (New York: Farrar, Straus and Giroux, 2010), 470.

[10] Heather McHugh, "Poise and Suspense." In *Poet's Work, Poet's Play: Essays on the Practice and the Art* (Ann Arbor, MI: University of Michigan Press, 2008), 277.

[11] Nicholas Carr, *The Shallows* (New York: W.W. Norton, 2011), 138.

[12] Stephen M. Fields, *Analogies of Transcendence: An Essay on Nature, Grace and Modernity* (Washington, DC: Catholic University of America Press, 2016), 1.

[13] Ibid., 25.

[14] Ibid., 69, 78.

[15] Amy Hungerford, *Postmodern Belief: American Literature and Culture Since 1960* (Princeton, NJ: Princeton University Press, 2010), xv.

[16] Ibid., xvi.

[17] William Lynch, *Christ and Apollo: Dimensions of the Literary Imagination* (New York: Intercollegiate Studies, 2003), 148.

[18] Teilhard de Chardin, *The Divine Milieu* (New York: Harper and Row, 1957), 78.

[19] The phrase is Rita Dove's as quoted by Helen Vendler in *The New York Review of Books* (November 24, 2011), 19. These broad orientations generally reflect the argument between the two over Dove's editorship of *The Penguin Anthology of Contemporary American Poetry*.

[20] Frank Kermode, *The Sense of an Ending* (Oxford: Oxford University Press, 1966), 56.

[21] W.H. Auden, *The Dyer's Hand*. (New York: Random House, 1990), 37.

[22] Ibid., 79–80.

[23] Ibid., 5.

[24] Randall Jarrell, *Poetry and the Age* (Gainesville, FL: University Press of Florida, 2001), 24.

[25] Ibid.

[26] Ibid., 74.

[27] T.S. Eliot, *Selected Prose of T.S. Eliot*. Ed. Frank Kermode (New York: Mariner Books, 1975), 37.

[28] Ibid.

[29] Ibid.

[30] Ibid., 39.

[31] Marilyn Nelson, "Owning the Masters." In *After New Formalism*. Ed. Annie Finch (Brownsville, OR: Story Line Press, 1999), 12.

[32] Ibid., 14.

[33] Ibid., 17.

[34] Agha Shahid Ali, "A Darkly Defense of Dead White Males." In *Poet's Work, Poet's Play*. Eds. Daniel Tobin and Pimone Triplett (Ann Arbor, MI: University of Michigan Press, 2007), 155.

[35] Kazim Ali, *The Rumpus* (September 9, 2015), http://www.therumpus.net.

[36] Ibid.

[37] Robert Pinsky, *Poetry and the World* (New York: Ecco Press, 1980), 122.

[38] Robert Patterson, "The Blues." In *An Exaltation of Forms*. Eds. Annie Finch

and Kathleen Varnes (Ann Arbor, MI: University of Michigan Press, 2002), 189.

[39] Langston Hughes, *The Selected Poems of Langston Hughes* (New York: Vintage, 1959), 33.

[40] Ibid.

[41] Quoted in Patterson, 189.

[42] Shahid Ali, 144.

[43] Ibid., 154.

[44] Derek Walcott, *The Poetry of Derek Walcott, 1948–2013* (New York: Farrar, Straus and Giroux, 2014), 237.

[45] Mary Jo Salter and John Stallworthy, Eds. *The Norton Anthology of Poetry* (New York: W.W. Norton, 1996), 58.

[46] Alice Meynell, Ed. *The Flower of the Mind* (London: Grant Richards, 1904), 101.

[47] *The Norton Anthology of Poetry*, 236.

[48] John Keats, *Bright Star: Complete Poems and Selected Letters* (London: Random House, 2009), 365.

[49] Elizabeth Bishop, *Poems* (New York: Farrar, Straus and Giroux, 2011), 214.

[50] Marianne Boruch, "Heavy Lifting." In *Poet's Work, Poet's Play*. Eds. Daniel Tobin and Pimone Triplett (Ann Arbor, MI: University of Michigan Press, 2007), 28.

[51] Auden, 78.

[52] Robert Pinsky, *The Situation of Poetry* (Princeton, NJ: Princeton University Press, 1978), 78.

[53] David Bentley Hart, *Beauty and the Infinite* (New York: Eerdmans, 2004), 7.

[54] Czeslaw Milosz, *The Witness of Poetry* (Cambridge, MA: Harvard University Press, 1984), 15.

[55] Ibid., 81.

[56] Hart, 133.

[57] Pinsky, *Situation*, 85.

[58] Milosz, 56.

[59] Wallace Stevens, *The Necessary Angel* (New York: Vintage, 1951), 130.

[60] Ibid., 174.

[61] Ibid., 175.

[62] Milosz, 56.

[63] Dorothea Lasky, "Ars Poetica," http://www.poetryfoundation.org.

[64] Anne Carson, *Decreation* (New York: Random House, 2005), 185.

[65] Weil, *Waiting for God* (New York: Harper Collins, 2009), 12.

[66] Ibid., 41, 42.

[67] Simone Weil, *The Need for Roots* (London: Routledge and Kegan Paul, 1987), 41.

[68] Ibid.

[69] Simone Weil, *A Simone Weil Reader* (New York: Moyer Bell, 2007), 350.

[70] Ibid., 354.

[71] Simone Weil, *Gravity and Grace* (New York: Routledge, 2002), 94.

[72] Ibid., 175.

[73] Weil, *A Simone Weil Reader*, 364.

[74] Ibid.

[75] Weil, *Gravity and Grace*, 148.

[76] Milosz, 114.

[77] Auden, 70–71.

[78] Weil, *Waiting for God*, 107.

[79] Weil, *Gravity and Grace*, 97, 117.

[80] Emily Dickinson, *Complete Poems,* Ed. Thomas Johnson (New York: Little

Brown, 1960), 280.

[81] C.K Williams, *Poetry and Consciousness* (Ann Arbor, MI: University of Michigan Press, 1998), 11.

[82] Weil, *A Simone Weil Reader*, 354.

[83] Dickinson, *Complete Poems*, 465.

[84] W.B. Yeats, *The Collected Poems of W.B. Yeats* (New York: Simon and Schuster, 1989), 193.

[85] Wallace Stevens, *Opus Posthumous* (New York: Alfred Knopf, 1989), 141.

[86] Weil, *A Simone Weil Reader*, 379.

[87] Ibid., 378.

[88] Ibid.

[89] Yusef Komunyakaa, *Neon Vernacular* (Middleton, CT: Wesleyan University Press, 1993), 159.

[90] Hart, 433.

[91] Ibid., 434.

[92] Ibid., 433.

[93] Pinsky, *Poetry and the World*, 3.

[94] Weil, *A Simone Weil Reader*, 378.

[95] Richard Wilbur, *The Collected Poems 1943–2004* (New York: Harcourt, 2004), 462.

[96] Weil, *A Simone Weil Reader*, 380.

[97] B.H. Fairchild, *The Art of the Lathe* (Farmington, ME: Alice James Books, 1993), 11.

[98] Louise Glück, *The Wild Iris* (New York: Ecco, 1993), 6.

[99] Weil, *Gravity and Grace*, 175.

[100] Marilynne Robinson, *Absence of Mind* (New Haven, CT: Yale University Press, 2010), 69.

[101] Janet Hobhouse, *Everybody Who Was Anybody: A Biography of Gertrude Stein* (New York: G.P. Putnam's Sons, 1975), 3.

[102] Ibid., 3–4.

[103] Ibid., 190.

[104] Ibid., 76–77.

[105] Ibid., 101.

[106] Ibid., 168.

[107] Ibid., 164.

[108] Ibid.

[109] Ibid., 166.

[110] Ibid., 168.

[111] Ibid., 225.

[112] Ibid.

[113] Gertrude Stein, *Wars I Have Seen* (London: B.T. Batsford, 1945), 4–5.

[114] Christopher Benfey, "The Alibi of Ambiguity," *The New Republic* (June 28, 2012).

[115] Lansing Warren, "Gertrude Stein's Views on Life and Politics," *The New York Times* (May 6, 1934).

[116] Quoted in Hobhouse, 211.

[117] Gertrude Stein, "Composition as Explanation." In *Gertrude Stein: Writings and Lectures 1909-1945*. Ed. Patricia Meyerowitz (New York: Penguin Books, 1967), 25.

[118] Ibid., 24.

[119] Ibid., 293.

[120] Hobhouse, 73.

[121] Stein, *Writings and Lectures*, 22.

[122] Augustine, *Confessions* (London: Oxford University Press, 2009), 231.

[123] Christine Casson, "Historical Narrative in the Lyric Sequence." In *The Contemporary Narrative Poem*. Ed. Stephen P. Schneider (Iowa City: University of Iowa Press, 2013), 130.

[124] Ibid., 133.

[125] Ibid., 142.

[126] Hobhouse, 78.

[127] Alfred Kazin, "Review of Composition as Explanation," *Reporter* (February 8, 1960).

[128] Gertrude Stein, *Tender Buttons* (San Francisco: City Lights Books, 2014), 33.

[129] Quoted in Hobhouse, 94.

[130] Tony Hoagland, *Real Sofistikayshun* (St. Paul, MN: Graywolf, 2006), 131.

[131] Hobhouse, 184–5.

[132] Ibid., 175.

[133] Stein, *Writings and Lectures*, 138–140.

[134] Ibid., 141.

[135] Ibid., 142.

[136] Robert Pinsky, *The Situation of Poetry* (Princeton: Princeton University Press, 1975).

[137] Paul Hoover, *Postmodern American Poetry II* (New York: W.W. Norton, 2009), xxvii.

[138] Ibid., xxix.

[139] Ibid., xliv.

[140] Paul Hoover, *Postmodern American Poetry*. First Edition. (New York: W.W. Norton, 2001), xxv.

[141] Ibid.

[142] Charles Olson, *Projective Verse* (New York: Totem Press, 1959).

[143] Hoover, *Postmodern American Poetry*, xvii.

[144] Hoover, *Postmodern American Poetry II*, xxxii.

[145] Ibid., liii.

[146] Ibid.

[147] Hoover, *Postmodern American Poetry*, xxx.

[148] Ibid.

[149] Charles Bernstein, *Content's Dream* (Chicago: Northwestern University Press, 1986), 61–2.

[150] Marjorie Perloff, *The Poetics in Indeterminacy* (Princeton, NJ: Princeton University Press, 1981), 73.

[151] Ibid., 85.

[152] Ibid., 98.

[153] Neil Schmitz, "Gertrude Stein as Postmodernist: The Rhetoric of *Tender Buttons.*" *Journal of Modern Literature* 3 (July 1975), 1206–7. Quoted in Perloff.

[154] See David Abrams's discussion of Maurice Merleau-Ponty in *The Spell of the Sensuous: Perception and Language in a More-than-Human World* (New York: Vintage, 1996), 73ff.

[155] Weil, *Gravity and Grace*, 152–153.

[156] Hoover, *Postmodern American Poetry II*, xxx.

[157] Pinsky, *Situation*, 3–4.

[158] Ibid., 115.

[159] John Ashbery, *Selected Poems* (New York: Penguin, 1985), 208.

[160] John Ashbery, *Self-Portrait in a Convex Mirror* (New York: Penguin, 1975), 43.

[161] John Ashbery, "Working Overtime." *The New York Review of Books* (January 11, 2009), 11.

[162] Louise Glück, "On Mannerism." *Metre* 7/8 (Spring / Summer, 2000), 121.

[163] Ibid, 124.

[164] Charles Bernstein, *Girly Man Chicago* (University of Chicago Press, 2006), 7.

[165] Ibid,140.

[166] Ibid, 57.

[167] Ibid, 117.

[168] Bernstein, *Recalculating* (Chicago: University of Chicago Press, 2013).

[169] Glück, 130.

[170] Gregory Wolfe, "Making it New," *Image* 81 (Summer 2014), 3.

[171] Anne Waldman, "Impossible Poetry." *American Poets: The Journal of the Academy of American Poets* 46 (Spring / Summer, 2014), 6.

[172] Waldman, 7.

[173] Glück, 130.

[174] Stein, 9.

[175] Thomas Sleigh, *Interview with a Ghost* (Minneapolis: Graywolf Press, 2006), 117.

[176] Ibid, 120.

[177] Ibid, 187.

[178] David Bentley Hart, *Atheist Delusions* (New Haven, CT: Yale University Press, 2009), 107.

[179] Ibid, 230.

[180] Wallace Stevens, *The Necessary Angel* (New York: Vintage, 195), 17.

[181] William Lynch, *Christ and Apollo* (New York: Sheed and Ward, 1960), 183.

[182] Gertrude Stein, *Everybody's Autobiography*, quoted in Lynch, 283.

[183] See Lynch, 214.

[184] Ibid.

[185] Owen Barfield, *Poetic Diction, Poetic Form: A Study in Meaning* (Hanover, NH: University Press of New England, 1973), 182.

[186] Lynch, 184.

[187] Ibid, 190.

[188] A.R. Ammons, *Set in Motion* (Ann Arbor, MI: University of Michigan Press, 1996), 13.

[189] Lynch, 195.

[190] Hart, 125–145.

[191] E.R. Dodds, *Pagan and Christian in an Age of Anxiety* (New York: W.W. Norton, 1965), 3.

[192] Elaine Pagels, *The Gnostic Gospels* (New York: Vintage, 1979), 19.

[193] The American Conference for Irish Studies, Dublin, Ireland. June, 2014.

[194] Pagels, 144.

[195] Dante Alighieri, *Inferno: A New Verse Translation by Michael Palma* (New York: W.W. Norton, 2002), 3.

[196] Jaroslav Pelikan, *The Emergence of the Catholic Tradition (100–600)* (Chicago: University of Chicago Press, 1971), 69.

[197] Matthew Dickman, *Flies* (Port Townsend, WA: Copper Canyon Press, 2011), 21.

[198] Ellen Bryant Voigt, "Double Talk and Double Vision," *Michigan Quarterly Review* (Summer 2009), 377.

[199] Ibid.

[200] Weil, *Waiting for God*, 107.

[201] Ibid.

[202] Tony Hoagland, *Real Sophistikayshun* (St. Paul, MN: Graywolf, 2010), 184.

[203] Stephanie Burt [originally published under the name Stephen Burt], *Close Calls with Nonsense* (St. Paul, MN: Graywolf, 2009), 13.

[204] Paul Ricoeur, *The Philosophy of Paul Ricoeur*. Eds. Charles E. Regan and David Stewart (Boston: Beacon Press, 1978), 99.

[205] Ibid., 132.

206 Ibid., 133.

207 Billy Collins, *Picnic, Lightning* (Pittsburgh: University of Pittsburgh Press, 1998), 74.

208 Dickinson, *Complete Poems*, 640.

209 Mary Oliver, *Devotions: The Selected Poems of Mary Oliver* (New York: Penguin, 2017), 50.

210 Rupi Kaur, *Milk and Honey* (New York: Andrews McMeel Publishing, 2015), 79.

211 Yeats, *Collected Poems*, 236.

212 Billy Collins, *Questions about Angels* (Pittsburgh: University of Pittsburgh Press, 1999), 20.

213 Mary Oliver, *New and Selected Poems Volume One* (Boston: Beacon Press, 1992), 34.

214 Yuval Noah Harari, *Sapiens: A Brief History of Humankind* (New York: Harper Collins, 2015), 356.

215 Elizabeth Alexander, "Introduction" in *The Essential Gwendolyn Brooks* (Washington, DC: Library of America, 2005), xiii.

216 Gwendolyn Brooks, *Blacks* (Chicago: Third World Press, 2001), 451.

217 Shahid Ali, 144.

218 Alexander, xiii.

219 Derik Smith, *Robert Hayden in Verse* (Ann Arbor, MI: University of Michigan Press, 2018), 18ff.

220 Robert Hayden, *Collected Poems* (New York: W.W. Norton, 1985), 5.

221 Robert Hayden, *Collected Prose* (Ann Arbor, MI: University of Michigan Press, 1984), 41.

222 Ibid., 12.

223 Ibid., 74.

224 Shahid Ali, 146.

225 Eileen Myles, "On the Death of Robert Lowell," *Wait* (June 27, 2011), http://

www.representimentaltumblr.com.

[226]Adrienne Rich, "Format and Form," in *After the New Formalism*. Ed. Annie Finch (Ashland, OR: Story Line Press, 1999), 6.

[227] Shahid Ali, 134.

[228] Natasha Trethewey, *Native Guard* (New York: Houghton Mifflin, 2006), 35.

[229] Laura Kasischke, *Poet's Work, Poet's Play*, 57–58.

[230] Burt, 17.

[231] R.S. Thomas, *Collected Poems 1945–1990* (London: Phoenix, 1993), 95.

[232] Ibid., 327.

[233] Ibid., 327.

[234] Ibid., 347.

[235] D.Z. Phillips, *R.S. Thomas: Poet of the Hidden God* (London: Wipf and Stock, 1986), 70.

[236] Thomas, *Collected*, 361.

[237] Quoted in Philips, 72.

[238] Thomas, *Collected*, 359.

[239] Ibid., 296.

[240] Ibid., 355.

[241] R.S. Thomas, *No Truce with the Furies* (London: Bloodaxe, 1996), 59.

[242] Ibid., 43.

[243] Ibid., 34.

[244] Thomas, *Collected*, 387.

[245] Ibid., 362.

[246] Ibid., 424.

[247] Ibid., 302.

[248] R.S. Thomas, *The Poems of R.S. Thomas* (Scottsdale, AZ: University of Arizona, 1985), 174.

[249] Thomas, *Collected*, 457.

[250] Thomas, *No Truce*, 62.

[251] Ibid., 29.

[252] Dennis O'Driscoll, *The Outnumbered Poet* (Loughcrew, Ireland: Gallery Press, 2012), 424.

[253] Hart, 241.

[254] Ibid.

[255] Stephen M. Fields, *Analogies of Transcendence* (Washington, DC: Catholic University of America Press, 2016), 79.

[256] Nicholas Carr, *The Shallows: What is the Internet Doing to Our Brains* (New York: W.W. Norton, 2011), 28–29.

[257] Ibid., 65.

[258] Ibid., 66.

[259] Wallace Stevens, *The Collected Poems of Wallace Stevens* (New York: Alfred A. Knopf, 1982), 358.

[260] Carr, 74.

[261] Ibid., 220.

[262] Robinson, 72.

[263] Hobhouse, 230.

[264] Thomas, *No Truce*, 33.

ABOUT THE AUTHOR

Daniel Tobin is the author of eight books of poems, *Where the World is Made, Double Life, The Narrows, Second Things, Belated Heavens, The Net*, the book-length poem *From Nothing*, and *Blood Labors. The Stone in the Air*, his suite of poems from the German of Paul Celan, appeared in 2018. Critical studies include *Passage to the Center: Imagination and the Sacred in the Poetry of Seamus Heaney* and *Awake in America*. He is the editor of *The Book of Irish American Poetry from the Eighteenth Century to the* Present, *Light in Hand: The Selected Early Poems of Lola Ridge, Poet's Work, Poet's Play: Essays on the Practice and the Art* (with Pimone Triplett), and *To the Many: Collected Early Works of Lola Ridge*. Among his awards are the "The Discovery/The Nation Award," The Robert Penn Warren Award, the Robert Frost Fellowship, the Katherine Bakeless Nason Prize, the Massachusetts Book Award in Poetry, the Julia Ward Howe Prize in Literature, and creative writing fellowships from the National Endowment for the Arts and the John Simon Guggenheim Foundation. He teaches at Emerson College in Boston.

ABOUT ORISON BOOKS

Orison Books is a 501(c)3 non-profit literary press focused on the life of the spirit from a broad and inclusive range of perspectives. We seek to publish books of exceptional poetry, fiction, and non-fiction from perspectives spanning the spectrum of spiritual and religious thought, ethnicity, gender identity, and sexual orientation.

As a non-profit literary press, Orison Books depends on the support of donors. To find out more about our mission and our books, or to make a donation, please visit www.orisonbooks.com.

Orison Books wishes to thank Lee Oser for his financial support of this book.

For information about supporting upcoming Orison Books titles, please visit www.orisonbooks.com/donate/, or write to Luke Hankins at editor@orisonbooks.com.